Ashley —

JOHN CROWLEY *with*

JENNIFER LILL-BROWN

Thanks for your

KNUCKLE

support

DRAGGING

SALES

A Primitive Process to Make More Money

KNUCKLE
DRAGGING SALES

Contact the authors if you would like information on how to access any and all programs or other materials associated with this book and its contents. This book may be purchased for educational, business, or sales promotional use.

For information or to order, please contact:

John Crowley
Knuckle Dragging Sales
923 Oldham Drive
Nolensville, TN 37135
(888) 666-1492
Email: info@knuckleds.com

WWW.KNUCKLEDRAGGINGSALES.COM

ISBN-13: 978-0-965-22012-5
Copyright© 2018 by Diversify Healthcare LLC
First Edition

Library of Congress Cataloging-in-Publication data on file
Library of Congress Control Number: 2018940024

Cover and interior design by Marisa Jackson
Original illustrations by Bryce Damuth

Printed in the USA

WHAT OTHER KNUCKLE DRAGGERS ARE SAYING

"Knuckle Dragging Sales is different . . . it's inspirational yet filled with common sense principles and tactics that will make you a more successful sales person . . . and a better person!"

—Carolyn D'Erasmo, National Sales Director, Kyowa Kirin, Inc.

"Crowley has provided a great read for anybody interested in sales or who thinks they are already a seasoned, knowledgable professional. I've been in sales and marketing for over 20 years, and too many elements resonated for me in his book—from how to be better organized and wiser in utilizing your time to creating value beyond just selling your product. I can vouch for his experiences from many shared phone calls over the years. His insights and honest approach provide a refreshing read, with a touch of humor. I highly recommend this book for anybody in sales."

—Brett Villagrand, Chief Commercial Officer, BC Platforms

"Crowley provides an excellent framework for what it takes to become the expert for your customer's business. If you desire to create customers for life, read *Knuckle Dragging Sales.*"

—Stephen Newell, Area Sales Manager, Medtronic Neurosurgery

"If you are looking for the next 'sales gimmick' this book is not for you. *Knuckle Dragging Sales* helps take proven techniques and ideas and adapt them in an ever-changing, new age of sales to become more successful professionals, leaders, individuals and, ultimately, better salespeople."

—Justin Smith, Vice President of Sales, Master Medical Equipment

"*Knuckle Dragging Sales* is a great book for a new salesperson like myself who wants to ditch the frustrating corporate robo-rep strategy for a personalized sales philosophy that yields greater job satisfaction and greater profits. If you haven't arrived at the realization that Crowley outlines the right way to sell, this book will feel like an epiphany. If you have, the book will put into writing what you've suspected has led to your sales success all along."

—**Chris Dingman,** Account Executive, Kelly Services Scientific Division

"John's book has something for everyone. . . . If you are new to sales, you will discover an intuitive mentor in its pages. If you are more experienced, or perhaps a bit weary in well-doing, John's words will inspire you to win again. . . . Not to win better, but to win differently. John's holistic approach results in success . . . with servitude and sincerity at its core. It's rare to have the opportunity to pick someone's brain with the experience that John Crowley has amassed. Soak it up. This book reads like the progression of a natural conversation between the experienced and the aspiring. I have been privileged to have the opportunity to put his valuable words into practice and I am already reaping the benefits and fruits of his labor. Thank you, John, for choosing to share your secrets and invest in the redefining of *the sales representative's reputation* as we strive to move towards creating and establishing long-term value for those we serve."

—**Claudia Friedman,** Medical Device Sales Consultant

"I would put *Knuckle Dragging Sales* with the best sales books I've ever read. Written by a salesperson for a salesperson, Crowley speaks my language. The use of real world trials and stories from Crowley's past made it personal. I felt like I was right there with the author and could relate to many of the situations he went through. I found myself laughing out loud on a crowded flight of people many times while reading. I'm excited to start my De-Evolution Revolution!"

—**Shaun Pasdon,** Sales Account Manager, Relypsa

"Crowley has crafted a fascinating exploration into the primal forces that drive us as sales professionals. *Knuckle Dragging Sales* is a must-read for the modern sales professional looking to engage customers with insight in the age of social media. *Knuckle Dragging Sales* provides an industry-transcending methodology for engaging customers with insight and providing value. Crowley provides a systematic methodology to provide value to our customers while maximizing our earnings. And be careful —beyond the emphasis on sales, this book might just make you a better person. If you finish this book and do not jump out of your seat to implement Crowley's methods, then you might want to see a doctor to check for a pulse. Crowley provides a window into the sales professional's psyche—how our most basic trait can propel us to succeed."

—**Andrew Voelker,** Global Account Manager, Gexpro Services; Best Selling Author of *Beneath the Greater Sky*

"'Big Red' provides you with time-tested, battle proven examples of sales success and strategies to implement in 'the greatest profession in the world.' He gives you the hard activities that only the best do—the core fundamentals for a highly successful sales career."

—**Cory Cairns,** Chief Development Officer, Team Rainmaker

"*Knuckle Dragging Sales* contains so many nuggets of wisdom that I will refer back to it when I feel stymied and cannot figure out what I am doing wrong or why the potential customer will not budge. What I liked most is its simplicity. There are so many books written that over-analyze the sales process and try to fit every sales rep and every customer into a box. Paralysis of analysis happens all too often. *Knuckle Dragging Sales* gets back to the basics, which is why the title is so apropos. Quit overthinking everything—be persistent, ask the right questions, shut up and listen and then figure out how to add value!"

—**John Wiley,** Surgical Equipment Specialist, Bausch + Lomb Surgical

"The amazing part about *Knuckle Dragging Sales* is the realization that such a broad group of people only need to invest a few hours of their day to generate disproportionate lifetime returns! Whether you are a brand new rep, a President's club vet, a struggling entrepreneur or a $1M company trying to break through a plateau—this book is for you. *KDS* taps into our primal motivations and breaks the key drivers of success into bite-sized chunks that can immediately be put into action."

—**Raymond Jebsen,** Vice President, CarePayment

"*Knuckle Dragging Sales* doesn't teach games, gimmicks, closing techniques or 'get rich quick' schemes. It makes it very clear that success is not easy, but it *is* simple. It gives you a competitive edge with its focus on mindset and execution skills that can be implemented in your process today to help you stand out from the sea of reps and catch your Big Fish."

—**John Stoothoff,** DPT and aspiring Medical Device Professional

"John Crowley is a captivating sales leader and author. I thoroughly enjoyed reading his book, *Knuckle Dragging Sales*. It was extremely motivating in my healthcare sales role. . . . The better you understand how your clients make money and what your prospects are incentivized to do, the faster you can get profitable deals done and reach your personal sales goals! Pick up this book if you want to be motivated to make more money this year. John Crowley instills a desire to chase after big goals because he practices what he preaches!"

—**Rebekah Panepinto,** Senior Director of Business Development, emids

"While so many books about sales are filled with theoretical concepts and complicated frameworks, *Knuckle Dragging Sales* was a breath of fresh air. From foundationally getting your head right, to goal setting and, ultimately, powerful execution, John delivers simple (not easy!) and actionable ways to get better at sales and make more money. He strips away the formality and delivers these insights honestly, with humility and with a killer sense of humor. This is a must read for anyone willing to do the work required to get better at sales!"

—**David Noonan,** Account Manager, Red Nucleus Learning Solutions

"Hard closing is a thing of the past. In this inspiring and witty guidebook, John will walk you through a simple and powerful sales philosophy that will enable you to take your sales results beyond what you ever thought possible. A must read for anyone truly serious about sales success."

—**Saul Marquez,** Regional Business Manager, Medtronic;
Host of Outcomes Rocket and Smart Medical Sales Podcasts

"The biggest problem with success in sales is we make it far more complicated than it should be and, as a result, too many fail. Success requires total commitment to doing the job—and all the hard work that comes with it. It requires focus, attention to detail and sharp execution. Focusing on your customer enables you to achieve your goals. John doesn't lay out magical formulas, he reduces selling to its essentials and outlines how sharp execution enables you to succeed."

—**David Brock,** CEO Partners in EXCELLENCE;
Best selling author of *Sales Manager Survival Guide*

"*Knuckle Dragging Sales* is real, raw, and essential. Crowley combines his inspiring story, insight from years of selling, and no-nonsense style to show you exactly how to win day in, day out in the sales profession."

—**Douglas Vigliotti,** bestselling author of *The Salesperson Paradox*

"After more than two decades in sales I've learned to loathe books on selling. *Knuckle Dragging Sales* is different. John Crowley's sales perspective comes from years carrying a bag, leading sales teams and learning by having his ass handed to him by a customer. Most importantly, it showed me how to rediscover the joy of the hunt."

—**Mark Schwab,** Deep Brain Stimulation-Therapy Consultant, Boston Scientific

"Crowley's simplistic approach to increasing sales, coupled with colorful examples, will help you immediately improve as a sales professional. He is a gifted storyteller, who through his own trials and tribulations will help you redefine yourself, add new tools and increase your motivation to get things done. My entire team will be receiving a copy."

—**Wes Watson,** Vice President of Business Development, VALiNTRY

KNUCKLE
DRAGGING
SALES

This book is dedicated to everyone who has ever invested in me. Your belief is what gave me the confidence to keep dragging my knuckles past fear.

To my girls—thank you for listening to my "ideas," supporting my "dreams" and encouraging my craziness.

Nads—you're more loved than you feel.

Doughy—you're braver than you believe.

Cheese—you're smarter than you will ever know. —*John*

To my husband, Will, and our phenomenal boys, Porter, Wyatt and Jesse. And to my parents, David (Papa) and Martha (Grandma). I am blessed to call myself wife, mom and daughter because of you incredible humans.

—*Jennifer*

TABLE OF CONTENTS

FOREWORD

I met John back in 1998 when he was a fresh-faced intern at Schein Pharmaceutical. There was something different about him. He had a unique competitive spirit and took on assignments that most in his class wouldn't have even thought about accepting. As his professional life and experience progressed, it was easy to see (and quite frankly remarkable to witness) him separate himself from the pack. John had an uncanny ability to see the core issue, task or deliverable that was required. He was one of those rare humans who could see both the forest *and* the trees.

John and I have spent many a day and night discussing that great, unanswered question: Why do some have enormous success in life, while others struggle through the challenges and never seem to get on top? In John's book, *Knuckle Dragging Sales*, he shows you how you can finally break through the excuses and win! In a world where the sales process has become complex, confusing and muddled, his process streamlines what is actually important from the noise. He reminds you to put the customer first, and the money will come.

The simplicity of the title says it all, doesn't it? Let's think about how terrifying it must have been to be a caveman—to provide for your family in the face of extreme adversity. As salespeople, we too have a daunting task—to provide for our families in the face of an ever-changing marketplace and growing competition (and do it all in a way that is scalable and teachable to others). John teaches us that if you develop a plan centered on what matters (your customer), executing that plan isn't just doable—it's *evolutionary!*

Those of us who spent our careers in selling know that if we aren't evolving, we're dying. We read books, go to seminars, watch videos and do anything we need to do to gain that edge. We have our own "cave wall scribbles" and acronyms meant to inspire and instruct. One of my favorites acronyms in this business is ABC, or "Always Be Closing." Thanks to its frequent use in the sales world (and thanks to Alec Baldwin in *Glengarry Glen Ross*), it has become overused and commonplace. Well, John took that outdated advice and evolved ABC into something real and relevant to salespeople today. Because of John Crowley, ABC now stands for "Accountable, Balanced and Consistent." To me, those three words define John, his business savvy and his acumen.

With so many different models for how to sell, it's refreshing to have it re-simplified. This book and its principles will not only improve your sales and closing ratio, but it will also take any task you think is impossible and help you craft a strategic plan to make it executable. I hope you enjoy this book as much as I did (Chapter Seven is a must read).

Jeff Lovesy

"The De-Evolution Revolution requires
you to ask yourself: *Am I willing to persist
long enough to help my customers
with more than just my product?*"

John Crowley

WHY ARE YOU HERE?

How many salespeople do you know who are millionaires? My guess is very few. Maybe none.

It's not hard to justify the low numbers. Frankly, most salespeople are *average* at best. From my experience, the majority of sales reps eventually get tired of spinning their wheels after a few meager attempts to sell. Then they quit because they're burned out after months of robo-dialing, failing to break past gatekeepers and making mediocre money.

That means that only a minuscule percentage of salespeople will ever achieve the kind of success that is widely promised in sales. I'm talking about six or seven figures in commission in just one year.

In fact, the percentage is so small that I know some of you reading this book will never reach that level. If you don't think you can commit to changing your ways, email us. We'll refund the money you spent on this book.

I want you to be one of the few who succeed, *but you've got to want it, too.* Do you want to know the difference between the rare millionaire success stories and all the rest?

Those rare successes are Knuckle Draggers.

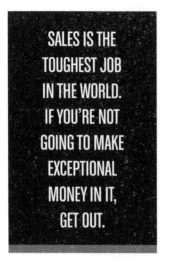

SALES IS THE TOUGHEST JOB IN THE WORLD. IF YOU'RE NOT GOING TO MAKE EXCEPTIONAL MONEY IN IT, GET OUT.

I know what you're thinking. "Isn't being a Knuckle Dragger a bad thing?"

That's a great question. Let me ask you something. Why are you reading this book? I know the answer—because you want to make more money.

You can tell yourself it's for a nobler reason. But no matter what your motivation is, you need money to achieve your goal. How can I be so sure? Because I know that, "I work to provide for my family" really means, "I work to make more money because kids are expensive."

I also know that, "I work so I can give back" is code for, "I work to make money so that I can afford to give back."

And let's not forget that, "I work to have the freedom to do what I want on my terms" translates to, "I work to make more money because money is what ultimately buys freedom."

Sales is money driven. It's all about the bottom line. If money is not important to you, you probably won't be in sales for long. The job is too tough to hang in there for any other reason.

For the lucky few who actually sell something they are truly passionate about, maybe their work is about more. But let's be real—most sales positions involve selling things that don't inspire passion. For most of us, the products we peddle are just a means to an end.

When you ask little kids what they want to be when they grow up, none will shout, "A commission-based salesperson!" Sales is not a glamorous job. Landing a sales gig isn't exactly hitting the career jackpot.

Throughout my career, I've been ignored, yelled at, spit on, chased by protestors and cussed out. I've slipped on ice and bruised my tailbone, pitted out a suit jacket on a sweltering August afternoon and split my pants chasing down a doctor. I've been called an overpaid caterer, an unreliable FedEx man, a glorified public relations rep and a legal drug dealer.

Yeah, definitely not a glorious gig.

So why am I here? And why are *you* here?

We're here for the money. We're here because sales is one of those rare professions that allows *you* to control the size of your paycheck and determine your own destiny.

Now back to your original question: Isn't knuckle dragging associated with stupidity, or at the very least, tacky, unpolished behavior?

Not at all. In fact, knuckle dragging represents the essence of getting back to what actually works in sales—SIMPLICITY.

During the eighties, some great business minds made a lot of money teaching people how to sell. They amassed a list of "tactics" that worked for them and saw a way to make money teaching these ideas to others.

Now, with the best of intentions, professionals in our industry try to convince the world to view sales as something it's not. Institutes teach "intricacies" of the sale. There are a thousand books with "101 closes for every conceivable selling scenario." Workshops dissect each possible micro-step in the sales process.

We've grown accustomed to hearing that sales is an "art form" and a "science." All of this while most salespeople still can't seem to get past the gatekeepers!

This is garbage.

Sales is not that complicated. It has little or nothing to do with your intelligence, your degree or your vernacular.

I asked the best salespeople what it takes to be successful. Do you know what they said? Things like "patience," "discipline," "charisma," "resilience" and "persistence."

What does every single one of those things have in common? They're *zero* percent science, and not one of them can be taught in a class! There are no courses in college called "Persistence 101" or "Fundamentals of a Winner's Attitude."

It really is all about dogged determination and persistence.

You persist and win—or you quit and fail.

You hunt and gather—or you starve and die.

Even a caveman could understand that.

When I tell people I'm a "knuckle-dragging sales guy," here's what I'm saying: I've simplified the sales game in a way that benefits my customers and makes me more money while doing it.

If you don't think you could ever view yourself as a knuckle-dragging salesperson, this book may not be for you. It requires a willingness to undergo a "de-evolution." It requires you to strip away preconceived notions and take a more simplified look at our profession.

You'll find me using the word *simple* a lot. But don't confuse simple with *easy*. Running is simple. Running a marathon is freaking hard! And sales is the marathon of professions.

If you're willing to think outside the tired and unoriginal sales box, rethink what this career is supposed to look like and fight for your success, I invite you to join the ranks of other Knuckle Draggers ...

Because it's time for a *De-Evolution Revolution!*

Rest assured that I *don't* want us to return to dwelling in caves or dragging relatives around by their hair. But I *do* want to strip away the fluff, the over-complication and the hyper-development of the sales process and get back to what really works.

No science. Just selling.

THE KNUCKLE DRAGGING SALES PROCESS

Before we get into the good stuff, let me give you a quick overview of this book. First, here are a few things that this book is *not*:

This is not a book of business buzzwords.

This is not a book filled with secret tips to success.

This book does not talk about soft sales science or sales art.

This book gives you simple, straightforward tactics to help you:

1. **Get your mind right.**

2. **Decide how to spend your time.**

3. **Understand what influences the decisions your customers make.**

There are two parts to the De-Evolution Revolution:

Part I: Reflection

Part I is about the mental game. You have to get your mind right and *think* like a successful salesperson before you can *act* like one. In the first few chapters, we'll define what motivates salespeople and lay the mental groundwork to take action.

Part II: Execution

In Part II, we'll discuss strategy and tactics. We'll talk about how to reach your biggest potential customers by:

1. Finding your way in the door.

2. Finding what motivates your customers to act.

You may be tempted to skip Part I and go straight to Part II. Don't. If you want the strategies in Part II to work, you need the foundation from Part I. In fact, Part I is far more critical to your success!

Again, this is not a book filled with secret tips, recipes or formulas. This is a knuckle-dragging sales *process*. A *formula* or *recipe* is a set of static, repetitive instructions. On the other hand, a *process* is a series of moldable actions (both mental and physical) used to achieve a particular end.

I'm all about action, whether it leads to success or a roadblock. And that brings me to what this book is really about:

Knuckle Dragging Sales **is about how to be different, not because you or what you sell is better, but because you're willing to persist until you win.**

As a salesperson and entrepreneur, I've been fortunate enough to succeed. But I know about failure, too. I've made lots of mistakes, some small, some enormous and many of them stupid. But I've never let those mistakes stop me. No matter what, I keep going.

You're going to fail sometimes. Some prospects will refuse to respond to your calls, emails or visits. Other prospects will say no matter what you try.

When the going gets tough, the average salesperson gives up.

The knuckle-dragging salesperson forges ahead.

Not sure if you have what it takes to become a knuckle-dragger? You only need one thing to begin. You need to have the type of determination that won't let you quit, no matter what crap comes your way. It can be scary, intimidating and sometimes feel impossible. But it is possible. Let's get started.

PART I:

REFLECTION

"Fear doesn't have to be taboo. Instead, use it as the ultimate fuel to spark your determination to win."

John Crowley

CHAPTER ONE

THE REAL REASON YOU'RE IN SALES

ommy Boy is one of the greatest comedies to ever hit the big screen. If you've never seen it, you're missing out. Poor, dimwitted Tommy Callahan (played by legend Chris Farley) is as lovable of an underdog as you can get.

When Tommy's dad unexpectedly dies, Tommy is left with tough choices concerning his father's auto parts plant. The bank has reneged on its loan and is demanding immediate repayment of all debts. Tommy must sell the company to their rival or try to save the plant himself.

The stakes are high. If he fails, Tommy will lose the business and his father's home, and every Callahan Auto Parts employee in their little town of Sandusky, Ohio will lose their job. If he succeeds, he saves the business, the jobs and his dad's legacy.

CHECK IT OUT ONLINE Tommy chooses to take the gamble, but it quickly starts to look like the wrong choice. His unprofessional antics alienate potential buyers left and right. Just when Tommy is on the verge of throwing in the towel, he wins over a surly waitress with an unlikely speech and realizes he's got what it takes to connect with potential customers. (Want to see the famous "chicken wings" scene? Check it out at www.knuckledraggingsales.com/book.) There are still a few snags to overcome, but in the end, Tommy succeeds at his goal.

Who doesn't love a good "triumph against all odds" story? We especially enjoy it when the endearing idiot outsmarts everyone and wins. Tommy was *determined* to win, and determination doesn't discriminate based on IQ.

Determination is the great equalizer in business. It's not about your education, your IQ or your background. More than anything else, success is determined by your willingness to just keep going.

Tommy was willing to do whatever it took to save his dad's company, and he didn't let the fact that it took him seven years to get a four-year college degree stop him.

People with that kind of fire in their belly are pretty rare these days. Especially in sales. Part of the problem is that sales isn't usually anyone's first choice of career. It's not like parents carefully groom their children from birth to be salespeople.

Nowhere in the world is there a mother saying to her daughter, "Now honey, you go to college and find yourself a good salesman to marry."

And yet according to the Bureau of Labor Statistics, there are over 14 million salespeople in this country alone.[1] That means that at least 11 percent of actively working people in the U.S. are in sales.

If no one aspires to be a salesperson, why do so many of us end up becoming one?

It's because of *fear*. More specifically, it's fear that stems from the uncertainty and anxiety of not having money—or our perception of not having enough money. This fear of poverty is called peniaphobia.

For two decades, I told myself that I was in sales for money. But once I really stopped to think about it, I realized I was in sales because I feared life without money.

I grew up the richest poor kid in town. My father was *terrible* with money. He made a good living but unfortunately believed that perceptions were reality. He was determined to make everyone believe we were far wealthier than we actually were. As a result, we lived in a 6,000-square-foot house but were too "house poor" to furnish it.

We belonged to the country club but couldn't afford proper attire for the clubhouse. When the seasons changed from cold to warm, we'd cut off our jeans and *boom!* Jorts were born. I once got kicked off the golf course for showing up in a pair of Jorts.

My mother had to feed four children (including two very big boys) on $100 a month. We routinely ran out of money before the end of the month. We were a ramen noodle family *long* before the cuisine became synonymous with broke college kids.

I remember the day my dad dropped me off at college (which I paid for myself). He went to the ATM but couldn't withdraw any money. I later found out the IRS had frozen his accounts for not paying taxes.

---

1   https://www.bls.gov/oes/current/oes410000.htm

Because my father earned a great income on paper but lived way beyond his means, I didn't qualify for any financial aid. During college, I was constantly stressed about how I was going to pay my tuition and room and board.

All of this fed my determination to never have to worry about money. I'd make sure my kids never needed anything the way I had.

Again, the key word is *determination* because that's what pushed me toward success when everything and everyone around me told me to give up. Remember, successful people aren't universally intelligent, well educated or well spoken. The one thing they *do* all have in common is determination.

Let's return to Tommy Callahan for a moment. Remember how determined he was to save his dad's company? What's fascinating is what *fueled* his determination. He was *afraid* of what would happen to all of those people who worked at the plant. He was *afraid* of letting them down. He was also *afraid* that people were right about him. He was *afraid* to fail miserably. Tommy unknowingly used his fear as fuel to overcome seemingly insurmountable odds.

Determination is the *fire* beneath us that propels us toward the win, and *fear* is the *gasoline* that sets the fire ablaze.

I know it's not popular, especially in the world of sales, to say that fear fuels motivation. But I'm not talking about living in a state of perpetual panic. I'm talking about using fear as a catalyst for getting off your ass and making that next sales call. Fear is an excellent motivator when you're feeling discouraged, dejected or just plain tired.

Think about fear. What comes to mind? Probably spiders or snakes— or, of course, public speaking. Have you ever wondered why people are so afraid to speak in front of a group?

Fear of public speaking isn't really about being up on stage. What we're afraid of is not being interesting enough and losing the audience's attention. We're afraid of sounding like an idiot. We're afraid of our inability to persuade other people to change their thoughts, habits, or beliefs.

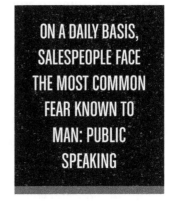

ON A DAILY BASIS, SALESPEOPLE FACE THE MOST COMMON FEAR KNOWN TO MAN: PUBLIC SPEAKING

That's what salespeople do every day! We're living that worst fear and calling it a career.

If you Google "fear," "fear and sales" and "fear and success," you'll get a whole slew of articles and posts about how to eradicate fear from your life. We've learned that it's wrong to feel fear. We've been led to believe that we're sabotaging our success by feeling an emotion that every single human being on the planet feels.

Fear is universal, but it's also taboo. A strange combination.

We've been taught to second-guess ourselves when we feel fear. The result? We believe that we have to be *fearless* in order to succeed. To me, that's even harder to pull off—and maybe even impossible for most people.

Fear is useful. It can make you braver. *After all, in the absence of fear, there is no such thing as bravery!* That's why I don't have a problem with fear. It's what kept Mr. and Mrs. Caveman from being eaten. The dread of living paycheck to paycheck has a distinct and useful purpose. It can provide the stimulus you need to push ahead, work harder and learn more when motivational quotes and vision boards aren't cutting it.

In sales, fear is a good sign that you're moving in the right direction. You know that panic that wells up inside of you

when you put aside busywork to go out and knock on doors? That's a good thing.

The presence of fear signifies that you're about to do something to advance your career and make more money.

What are you afraid of? Whatever it is, don't pretend it's not there. Instead, acknowledge it—and then use it as fuel to ignite a raging inferno of determination.

WHY YOUR WHY ISN'T WORKING

To get you moving in the right direction, we need to talk about what *really* motivates you. I know what you're thinking. If that's the case, why have I been focusing on fear? There's a method to my madness. Stick with me.

Most people would agree that the most recognized and acceptable motivators are the "things" we want in life: cushy retirement, the ability to give back, college fund, fancy car, fancy house and more. While *your* motivation and *my* motivation may look a little different on the surface, they're all made of the same thing. Peel back a few layers and you'll see Ben Franklin's smirking, green $100 face.

Don't be ashamed of this. Do you know how the world's greatest philanthropists effect change and shape people, policies and the planet? They have the means to pay for all of the resources required to make it happen.

Do you know how to provide a better life for your kids and leave a legacy? I'm sure you know, but I'll say it anyway—the more resources you have at your disposal, the better chance they have to succeed.

Money stacks the odds in your favor and increases your chances of getting a leg up in life. That's why we've got to get our minds right and focus on what *really* gets us up and moving in the morning.

I know this is not a popular message. What's far more accepted are the words of great speakers and authors. Look at Simon Sinek. In his book *Start with Why*, he states that "profit (money) is not a why, but rather it's a byproduct." To him and others, money is not a why or even a goal, but merely a tool to achieve peace, find security, attain freedom or fill ourselves with pride for a job well done.

Wait. So those feelings of peace, security and pride are supposed to be my why?

That question plagued me for a while. Here's what bugged me about it—most steady jobs produce those outcomes. If you don't live beyond your means, a "normal" occupation will provide you with security. If you're smart with your income, a "normal" profession will enable you to set savings aside. You can take pride in what you do and feel satisfied.

> **DOES YOUR WHY KEEP YOU DRAGGING YOUR KNUCKLES PAST ALL THE OBSTACLES IN A SALES CAREER?**

These justifications may work for some, but I don't believe they work for those of us brave (or maybe stupid) enough to go out and sell every day. In other words, those reasons alone are not sufficient enough to justify choosing *the hardest job on the planet*.

Sales is unlike any other profession. You don't need a formal license to sell (except in the financial or insurance industry). You don't need special schooling. Hell, in many cases you don't even need a degree. I've hired people with GEDs and MBAs for the same position!

If sales is an undesirable job that nobody ever dreams of doing, why are so many candidates lined up outside the door? Simon is partly right—making money isn't a why. But fear of not having money absolutely is.

We fear the embarrassment that comes from not having enough in the bank to pay the bills.

We fear having to tell our kids that we can't afford to go on any vacations.

We fear that we aren't as happy as everyone else is (at least according to what we see on social media). Twenty-year-olds are posting Instagram selfies from money-filled gold bathtubs, and we suddenly find ourselves stressing about the lack of gold bathtub in our own bathroom.

Most of us either have no degree or naïvely chose a useless degree like Communications, Marketing or Political Science. When it comes time to get a job, we're faced with two options:

1. Find a job with a starting salary of $30,000 a year and top out at $59,124[2] a year.

2. Get a job in sales and create your own destiny.

See? As it turns out, it's fear that pushes us away from the brainless, gutless nine-to-five desk job and causes us to "go big or go home."

Unfortunately, there's a downside to fear. A lot of people go into sales because they think it's an easy job where you can make a ton of money quickly (we've all seen the ridiculous ads that promise $10K or more a month to "be your own boss" and "work part-time").

To these fortune seekers, a sales job is a get-rich-quick scheme that comes with business cards. If you have a good personality, people will like you and buy from you, right? All you have to do is talk to people and the rest will take care of itself, right?

No! In fact, this common misconception is exactly why:

- There's such a high turnover rate in sales.

- There's such a negative perception of sales reps.

- There are so many dejected salespeople.

---

2   Source: https://www.aol.com/article/finance/2017/03/01the-average-salary-by-education-level/21864723/

- There are so many ineffective salespeople.

- There are so few salespeople who invest in themselves.

These big dreamers got into sales for a compelling enough reason—fear—but when they learned that sales is a hell of a lot harder than they expected, they didn't harness the power of that fear and failed to push through.

The worst part? The lack of determination in these uninspired, unprepared robo-reps is ultimately why our buyers are annoyed, avoid us like the plague and have turned to the Internet to educate themselves.

I don't care where you're from, how high your IQ is or how educated you are—there's no such thing as easy money. We all want it. We all want more of it. We all have good reasons for wanting more of it. We have family to support, places we want to go and people we want to help.

And it's terrifying to think we might not get to realize those dreams.

Being *fearless* isn't about eliminating all fear from your life. That's an impossible task, anyway. Being fearless is about harnessing fear's power and using it to propel forward!

The Neanderthals weren't fearless. They had plenty of fear. It kept their bellies full and their children alive. They were also brave. But being fearless isn't the same thing as being brave.

Bravery is when you push ahead despite fear. The best salespeople are brave. More importantly, they know how to harness the power of their fear and use it as fuel to fire their determination.

Fear is too valuable to ignore. It's a priceless tool that every knuckle-dragging salesperson should utilize to keep fighting and to win.

"Your brain is ready to be molded into
a knuckle-dragging sales machine.
But you've got to do the work, keep learning,
never quit and stop hanging out with losers."

John Crowley

CHAPTER TWO

THE FIGHTER INSIDE

Tommy Callahan was a guy who felt fear and kept fighting. Everyone assumed he would fail. He was constantly knocked down. Even Richard (his road trip companion who was supposed to be on his side) thought he was a complete imbecile. He dealt with internal doubts and external criticism.

I get Tommy.

I'm no scholar. I always did "okay enough" in school to keep moving forward. I was a good athlete but worked hard to stay that way. I didn't go to an Ivy League college and had a pretty lousy GPA until I discovered business classes.

My resume reads like a work of science fiction. Here's the gist: I went from being a low-level pharmaceutical sales rep to failing in a business start-up to becoming a top-level executive at a Fortune 26 company to becoming an author, speaker and sales coach.

Now that's a career progression that makes *perfect* sense (not).

My path to the present day doesn't look pretty by anyone's standards. Luckily, success in sales is not determined by any societal measuring stick.

It's about the primitive fighter inside you.

Tommy faced his fair share of fears, but the difference between failure and sweet victory was what he did with it. He was propelled by his fears to keep going.

AN UNEXPECTED BATTLE

Throughout my career, I have seen the fighter's spirit in so many cancer patients. Cancer is unquestionably one of the things in life that people fear most. Of my 20 years in healthcare sales, I've spent 15 of those in oncology. Although not always the case, I've noticed that a lot of the people who successfully beat the odds of the disease have an unmistakable fight inside them that keeps them pushing past the fear.

No one likes talking about cancer. Some call it the "c word," as though saying the actual word out loud will summon the cancer cells from their slumber and cause them to multiply.

Call it irony, poor lifestyle choices or just bad luck, but at the age of 30, I found out that I (a non-smoker who had never swallowed paint chips or inhaled asbestos as a kid) had lung cancer.

Before the diagnosis, I took my good health for granted. I had been a college athlete and was always in great shape. After spending the first few years of my post-college existence living the cushy life of a pharmaceutical sales rep working a small territory, I started working in the world of oncology drug distribution. I went from representing pharmaceuticals that sold themselves (like Viagra) to selling the *exact same* drugs as my competition for the same price.

In short, the only competitive advantage I had was . . . me.

In oncology drug distribution, the winner is the sales rep who can offer more value by providing better service to customers. I instinctively understood this, and as a result, I crushed this new position.

Don't get me wrong—the job sucked. But that was less about the job and more about the company I was working for. If this company had an unofficial slogan it would be, "Do whatever it takes. No, really. Whatever it takes."

While I didn't do "whatever it took," I did work myself into the ground. My once tiny territory had expanded into three states, which meant I was constantly on the road. I left Monday morning and came home late Thursday night. It was hell on my wife, Amy, and our two young daughters.

Within two years, I went from weighing 220 pounds to tipping the scale at 318 pounds. I slept just a few hours a night. One night a week I would pull an all-nighter. Eventually, my body started rebelling against the assault. It was as if my cells were saying, "A hundred pounds in two years? No sleep? Seriously?"

My damaging lifestyle habits finally manifested themselves. Over the course of six months, I got pneumonia five times. Unfortunately, every time I became symptomatic, I was on the road. I ended up in random emergency rooms or mini clinics where they always followed the same protocol: order an x-ray to confirm the pneumonia and a CT scan to determine the cause.

Unfortunately, because lungs are really dense and deep inside our bodies, the doctors I saw couldn't identify the culprit. And so the cycle continued. I'd get symptomatic. They'd put me on an antibiotic. I'd improve and be able to function. I'd never totally get better.

The fifth bout started in Missouri. I got pneumonia and went to the ER, where they performed a CT scan and finally saw something (a "speck" is the term they used). I drove home to Nashville and had a bronchoscopy. The test revealed a big, nasty carcinoid tumor in my right lung.

Amy and I began the process of trying to find the right surgeon. Before long, a surgeon presented the idea of cutting the tumor out and stitching the remaining lung back together—like a Franken-lung. The procedure would leave me with reduced lung capacity, but 1.4 lungs are better than only one lung.

This idea sounded great in theory. In reality, the only one willing to do the surgery was the rudest, most arrogant surgeon ever. Let's call him Dr. Bedside Manner. We had initially ruled him out, but after meeting with doctor after doctor who lacked the right experience to perform the complicated resection, we came crawling back to Dr. B.M.

The surgery was scheduled for Valentine's Day. As they rolled me off to the operating room, Dr. B.M. casually informed us, "So, there's a one-in-20 chance of you dying. But knock on wood, I've never had anybody die on the table."

Amy stopped him. "When *have* you had people die?"

As if telling us where to go for the best pizza, he said, "Post-surgery. From pneumonia."

That's just what your wife wants to hear as they wheel you away to cut you open.

After a four-hour surgery turned into a nine-hour operation, Dr. B.M. didn't even come out and tell Amy that it was over and I had survived. He went right into his next surgery and left her sitting alone, thinking the worst.

On top of all that, the hotshot surgeon didn't even sew the bottom piece of lung to the top. He just lopped it off. So I was left with one functioning lung and a little nubbin for the other.

But the worst was over, right? Nope! On day two of my recovery in the hospital, "it" happened.

I got pneumonia, and it was brutal, at least according to Amy. Between the surgery and the painkillers, it was all a blur for me. She was the one who battled with the doctors over the best course of action.

The entire ordeal was terrifying, but here's the craziest part:

It never once dawned on me that I might not make it. I didn't lie there and accept defeat. Somehow my instinctual response was, "I don't know how, but I'm going to make something good come out of this."

> KNUCKLE DRAGGERS CHOOSE TO NEVER QUIT. AS A RESULT, THEY KEEP GOING WHEN EVERYONE ELSE CAN'T OR WON'T.

I didn't go into surgery believing I'd die. When I got pneumonia a few days later my first thought wasn't, "This is it. I'm not going to make it."

The fight was just *in* me. Quitting wasn't an option. You can call it the "law of attraction" or something similar, but I think it's simpler and less cliché than that.

When you're faced with a roadblock, crisis or task, you have a choice—you can be the kind of person who sits and waits for the inevitable fall of the axe or the kind that forges ahead in spite of fear.

I forged ahead. In fact, losing my lung became the catalyst I needed to change my life. I had felt the fear of being told I might not get to see my girls grow up and used that as fuel to blaze a new path. Why did it cost me a body part? I'll never know. I *do* know that we can't choose the moments that change us.

I recovered and went home. Six months later, I was declared cancer-free. But from the moment I left the hospital, I vowed to change my life one piece at a time.

First and foremost, I fixed my lifestyle habits. I quit drinking, started eating right and addressed my sleeping issues. It took almost two years of early mornings at the gym and a massive overhaul of my diet, but I finally got into good shape and felt great again.

It's a constant battle to stay healthy. It's also a fight to stay at the top of the mountain in sales. There's always some hotshot newcomer ready to encroach on your territory and claim your spot.

How badly do you want to retire at 50? How badly do you want to leave a financial legacy? These are the types of questions you need to answer before you can reach your breakthrough and take advantage of the fear we all naturally feel.

You can't choose all of your battles. But you can choose how to approach your battles, whether it's a cancer diagnosis or a sales call. Call it a "knuckle-dragging outlook," but I never assume I won't succeed.

I am not naïve. I know there are plenty of worst-case scenarios that can and will arise. The difference is that I assume there's an unconventional or novel way to win the battle. And I believe that I'm just the person to attain that victory.

YOU MIGHT NEED A NEW BRAIN

Are some people natural born fighters? Probably. But there's still hope for those of us who aren't. You can train your brain to do anything.

When you want to change the way you eat, you have to retrain your taste buds. It works the same way for your brain. Have you ever heard of *neuroplasticity*? (I know I promised there wouldn't be any science in this book, but I was talking about the "science of selling," so this doesn't count.) There is a renowned neuroscientist named Dr. Michael Merzenich who gave a TED talk in 2004 entitled "Growing Evidence of Brain Plasticity." (Want to watch it? Check it out at www.knuckledraggingsales.com/book.)

CHECK IT OUT ONLINE

According to Merzenich, the commonly accepted idea that the adult brain is hard-wired and incapable of change after childhood is incorrect. Here's how Merzenich explains it in his book, *Soft-Wired: How the New Science of Brain Plasticity Can Change Your Life:*[3]

> What recent research has shown is that under the right circumstances, the power of brain plasticity can help adults' minds grow. Although certain brain machinery tends to decline with age, there are steps people can take to tap into plasticity and reinvigorate that machinery.

He goes on to explain the "right circumstances" that are able to revamp our aging brains: engaging in focused, hard work, paying attention, determining to succeed and maintaining overall brain health.

How convenient is it that all of these traits are the *exact same* ones that make salespeople successful?

Luckily, it doesn't take a neuroscientist to understand this concept. In caveman terms, it's never too late to teach an old dog new tricks (or in this case, new mindsets).

> THE MORE YOU DO SOMETHING, THE MORE YOUR BRAIN REMEMBERS EACH PAST ATTEMPT, MAKES ADJUSTMENTS AND GRADUALLY IMPROVES.

---

3   Merzenich, Michael M. *Soft-wired: how the new science of brain plasticity can change your life.* San Francisco: Parnassus, 2013. Print.

If the brain remains open to change, then no matter what kind of mindset you have today, you can retrain your brain to adopt the mindsets needed to win in sales. Here are a few of the basic principles Merzenich outlines in his book:[4]

1. **Get your game face on.** Staying alert and ready for change makes it possible for your brain to be retrained. Going through the motions at work—or switching to autopilot as we salespeople often do—closes off the brain to any remodeling opportunities. Keeping your foot on the gas pedal fires up your brain and tells it that you're ready to learn.

2. **Practice, practice, practice.** Our coaches were right—practice really does make perfect. The constant repetition of the right activities is what eventually changes your brain and causes key behaviors and mindsets to stick. Repetition is essential because your brain sees actions and attitudes as temporary until they significantly alter an outcome in your life (for better or worse).

3. **Don't stop studying and reading.** You've probably heard this before, but it's worth repeating. If this is one of the first books you've read since college, thank you, but your brain wants more. Learning drives your brain cells to work together and makes you more productive.

4. **Starve the bad stuff.** Whenever your brain is focused on improving a skill, it's weakening the connections of neurons that aren't being used at that moment. What does that mean? The less you indulge in unproductive activity and negative trains of thought, the less it will interfere with your mind's more important and lucrative work.

---

4   Hampton, Debbie. "Neuroplasticity: The 10 Fundamentals Of Rewiring Your Brain." October 28, 2015. Accessed via http://reset.me/story/neuroplasticity-the-10-fundamentals-of-rewiring-your-brain/.

5. **There's always a downside.** As with every great power, there's a flipside. Just as you can retrain your brain to think and act in ways that will make you more successful, it's just as easy to generate negative changes, too.

That last one is particularly important. And it's not just about you—it's also about who you surround yourself with. Do you associate with people who are always playing the victim? We all know people who aren't successful because "the other salespeople have better territories" or "the market is just too volatile right now" or "I never get the good products."

If you're around people who talk like this, you'll eventually start thinking this way as well. Surround yourself with people who think like winners.

To paraphrase Merzenich's brilliant ideas: *stay alert, work hard, don't quit, keep learning, turn off the television and stop hanging out with losers.*

Do that, and your reward will be a mind that makes you more money.

No matter your IQ, your brain is ready to impress you with its abilities. If you find the daily grind exhausting, it doesn't always have to be that way. If you get easily discouraged, take no's personally or have a hard time staying on track after the fifteenth gatekeeper in a row brushes you off, those reactions and mindsets don't have to be the ones you always have.

The Neanderthals were never promised a single meal. They were hungry most of the time. More often than not, they set out hunting for food and came back empty-handed.

After a long day of hunting and gathering a whole lot of nothing, do you think they sat down next to the fire, threw up their hands and said, "This sucks, I quit"?

Do you think they let overwhelming hunger pangs and freezing winters stop them? Not by a long shot. Resolve to be like those cavemen and let nothing stand in your way. Your brain can still be molded into a success-minded, gatekeeper-crushing machine.

"There are no valid reasons
for not succeeding in sales.
There are only excuses for
not persisting."

John Crowley

CHAPTER THREE

KNUCKLE DRAGGING ATTITUDE

If you think success in sales is easy, I want you to put down this book and go do something else. Maybe color. Maybe sing some songs. Or just take a nap. You've earned it, snowflake. Send us an email and we'll get you your money back (because it looks like you'll be needing it).

If you're still with me, I know you want to be part of that elite group of people who achieve real success in sales. This group is willing to do whatever it takes to reach their goals, and they want it so badly that nothing can stand in their way. These are the professionals I want to be around, teach and learn from. They are the people who will hold me accountable for my actions and make me better in every way.

We should be surrounding ourselves with other Knuckle Draggers. They're the type of people who don't let things like soul-sucking rejection stand in their way. They put their heads down and persist, aided by the right attitude.

Before I start to preach about the importance of attitude, let me say I'm a recovering shitty attitude-aholic. Just like any other addiction, it's difficult to fight "bad attitude" peer pressure. To this day, there are times when I find myself relapsing.

> IT'S TOUGH TO SHAKE A BAD ATTITUDE. LIKE AN ADDICTION, IT TENDS TO CREEP BACK WHEN YOUR GUARD IS DOWN.

Looking back on my life, it's easy to see that when I experienced the largest commission checks, the fastest and most significant promotions and the biggest advances in my personal life—all of those moments had one thing in common.

I had a positive attitude.

When I got myself into the deepest pit of my life, neglecting my health and happiness, I had a cancerous attitude. After my actual cancer went into remission, I decided to fix my career. In the seven years prior to my diagnosis, I had been working for a company I hated. I had no respect for my superiors or the company's culture. It was a challenge to get out of bed in the morning.

Making a horrible situation worse, there was zero upward mobility. I was miserable and didn't see a way to evolve my career.

I realized that even if you have the right motivation to work, if you don't believe in your company or what you're selling, you'll never be satisfied with your career.

I made a leap of faith and accepted a job working for another company in oncology. Two of my closest colleagues made the switch as well. With the prospect of starting fresh, the three of us were filled with the kind of enthusiasm we hadn't felt in years.

Only one thing worried me: I had signed a non-compete with my previous employer. I consulted with my lawyers about this being a problem, but they assured me that it wouldn't be.

My employer saw it much differently.

From their perspective, this new company swooped in and poached three of their best salespeople. They were going to make us pay dearly for our treachery. And they did, in the form of four separate $10 million lawsuits—one for each of us and one for the company.

Our lawyers told us there was a good chance we'd win in court, but it would take countless dollars and years of litigation. I was pissed. But eventually I conceded. Suddenly I found myself unemployed and blackballed. It was ugly. I couldn't get a job anywhere in the vicinity of healthcare.

During this dark period, I made decisions based on anger, hatred and spite. Rarely did it turn out well for me. Even worse, it negatively impacted my family.

I didn't realize it at the time, but in retrospect I can see I was taking the easy road. Like everything else worthwhile in life, having the right attitude can be extremely hard. It's easy to complain. It requires zero intellectual energy. That's why the laziest and least motivated among us spend all their time whining about quotas and territories.

Once they're allowed in, bad attitudes spread like pink eye through a kindergarten classroom. One person can literally bring down an entire team, division or even an organization.

    Unfortunately, attitude is not a zero sum game. You need many good attitudes to overcome the damage just one bad attitude can cause.

Having the right attitude means finding a solution rather than adding to the problem. It means being more like the honeybee and less like the seagull. Honeybees are an underappreciated yet pivotal part of our ecosystem. They are responsible for pollinating the crops that feed 90 percent of the world. Without the honeybee, the planet would struggle to support the human population.

Then there is the seagull. Aside from being the occasional shark snack, all seagulls do is crap. What's worse is they fly in, steal your picnic, crap and then leave. That's what people with negative attitudes do—they complain about everything that's wrong, offer zero solutions, rob the team of its momentum and eventually quit.

I aim to be someone who contributes to success (a honeybee), not someone who undermines it (a seagull). That resolve is a daily decision that only you can make. It's not easy, but when you have the right attitude on an ongoing basis, the floodgates of opportunity open up.

THE GLASS-HALF-EMPTY PATH TO SUCCESS

Are there people who naturally have the right attitude *all* the time? Maybe. But I've never met any of them.

The right attitude is a choice. Like everything else in sales, it's not complicated—but it's also not easy. You must wake up every day and consciously decide if you're going to own the day or if the day will own you.

I'm not talking about an eternally optimistic, naïve attitude. Believing that everything will always come up roses is one of the fastest paths to disappointment. In fact, hoping for the best and never expecting the worst will almost always lead to an unsuccessful sales career. Here's a reality check:

You will get punched in the face. It will hurt.

How do you move past this harsh truth and keep dragging your knuckles until you succeed?

Whether you toughen up or crawl into your safe space depends on the expectations you set. If you expect a job that pays a ton of money to be easy, you're delusional. You'll also continue living paycheck to paycheck. If you expect to always get the sale with no objections, you'll be devastated when you don't. Expect roadblocks. Also expect to be able to figure out a way past them.

You also need to decide how you want to learn the tough lessons that a sales career offers. There are two ways to learn in this profession—*experience* and *exposure*.

Believe me when I say that exposure is the better option.

Negative experience upon experience can destroy a sales career, while exposure to the right ideas, systems and mindsets allows you to sidestep some of the massive disappointments that lead to failure.

If you have a toxic attitude, associate with people who display toxic behaviors, or operate with your head in the sand, you'll eventually look back and see the correlation of your unproductive attitude to the unproductive outcomes you've experienced. The most prevalent toxic behavior in sales is excuse-making. The excuse makers are easy to spot—their failures are always someone else's fault. These people are also often jealous of the success of others and lash out with reasons why that success wasn't merited.

On the other hand, if you expose yourself to successful people, you'll quickly see that conscious determination isn't a "nice to have." It's a "must have" if you want to achieve great success. The rock stars of the sales world don't place blame. They don't belittle the success of others. They see their mistakes, learn from those mistakes, and they're better for it. Then they pass that wisdom along to others.

Having the right attitude isn't about imagining that all your customers are going to say yes. It's not about believing with all your heart that your product is superior. What is the right attitude for a salesperson? It looks a little different for everyone, but ultimately it's about being able to answer yes to one question: *Do I believe in myself enough to keep going?*

Do you believe that the worst-case scenario can and will happen, and when it does, you won't be defeated?

Ironically, I think pessimistic people have the best attitude for succeeding in sales. If you approach a situation by imagining the worst thing that could happen, you'll realize that the worst case is really not so bad. Then you have nowhere to go but up.

This is exactly how I deal with stress, and for me, worst cases often lead to the best outcomes.

When I started my first company, I knew that 95 percent of new businesses fail in the first year. Who in their right mind would quit a high-paying job to start a company that is highly likely to take a nosedive within the first 12 months?

To further stack the odds against me, I had zero experience working with start-ups. My wife was a stay-at-home mom. We weren't wealthy. Oh, and I had just liquidated my savings to pay for legal bills, thanks to the non-compete lawsuit.

It was a gamble that put my family at risk. Would we have to sell the house? Would we be able to find a place to rent in the same school district to minimize the impact on the kids' lives? Would I work so much that I'd miss important moments with the girls?

I kept telling myself that the absolute worst case scenario would be failing. But at least I'd learn more in six months than I had in 15 years in a deadbeat sales job. If I had to go back to sales, at least I'd have a fresh outlook.

After my start-up floundered for a while, I needed to find some source of income to keep us afloat. I started consulting. One of those consulting gigs brought me to a big corporation that was suffering from a malignant corporate culture. They thought they needed a new sales model. Forget restructuring—they needed a completely new attitude.

The CEO told me, "These people whine about everything. One employee just complained that we only gave him one week of paid vacation between Christmas and New Year's."

Paid!

I explained that it's human nature to complain. The key to moving past our complaining nature is to compare our complaint to the worst case scenario and realize it can always be worse.

The example I always use is the time I was consulting for a company and also acting as their interim COO. One morning the CEO called me and said, "We can't make payroll."

She told me to deliver the news to the team of eight. *Ok, I can handle that. It's just a temporary glitch, right?* Then she added, "Also effective immediately, everyone will be brought down to a base of $25K plus commission."

Present salaries ranged from $80K to $150K, but that wasn't even the biggest issue. The real problem was that she didn't have a single salesperson on the team. They were all operational roles with no way to generate commission.

Imagine the conversations that followed.

"Hey Chad, I appreciate all you do for the company, but I have some bad news. You know how we used to pay you $150K? Well, all we can afford now is $25K. Oh, and if you're thinking about quitting, I'd advise against it because we need you to do your job so we can get paid by our customers. If you quit now, we can't pay you what we already owe you."

That kind of conversation makes the "only one week of paid vacation between Christmas and New Year's" problem seem pretty insignificant.

You've probably heard the phrase, "Hope for the best but expect the worst." I live that every day, at least the last part of it. Before each sales call, I prepare myself for every conceivable bad outcome.

I prepare to get shut down by the gatekeeper.

I prepare to be told, "Sorry, it just comes down to price."

I prepare to hear that I'm losing the business before walking into an existing customer's office.

Does it sound like I'm expecting to fail? Not at all. Expecting to fail and being prepared to fail are two entirely different things. When you're prepared to fail, any outcome better than a worst-case scenario ends up feeling like a success. Sometimes you even come out on top.

Everyone experiences a worst-case scenario at some point in their career. It's up to you whether you're going to be prepared for it or not.

ONE KNUCKLE DRAGGER'S ATTITUDE ROUTINE

As sales professionals, we have many aspects to our jobs. Not only are we responsible for keeping our pipelines full, we also must move active leads through the pipeline and transform them into money on the other side.

Without a process, it's chaos. And for a salesperson, chaos means letting dollars slip through the cracks.

My process starts with attitude and mindset preparation. It's the most important part of my day. In fact, my entire routine breaks down without it. Here is a rundown of my daily mindset prep:

1. **Prepare the night before.** My day begins at night. Too many people waste valuable time in the evening watching TV, playing video games or doing mindless crap on their phones. Our ancient ancestors didn't have TVs or electricity. They went to bed when the sun went down. When the sun rose, they got up and got shit done. I cut out TV five years ago and it dramatically changed my life. I go to bed early so I can wake up early.

Maybe it's a placebo effect, but I honestly believe that "early to bed, early to rise" gives me swagger. When I hear that someone was out partying all night, I internally grin because I know that I'll be more focused and sharper than him all day. I see it as an opportunity to separate myself from the pack.

2. **Work out and meditate.** After I wake up, I head to the gym. Before walking in, I spend ten minutes meditating in my car. I don't use that word often because it freaks people out. They think I'm a hippie pothead. Call it "mental preparation" if that makes you feel better. I use the *Headspace* app, which is the best tool I've found. Thanks to the app, I've turned meditation into a consistent habit.

3. **Review your goals.** After I get my mind prepped, I open my goal progression spreadsheet on my phone and pick one thing that I'll do that day to advance my BHAG (Big Hairy Audacious Goal). This keeps me focused on what's important and prevents me from getting sidetracked. In the past, I would chase unicorns that didn't help with my BHAG. This routine helps tremendously with focus.

4. **Set appointments for every step.** I have daily appointments set in my calendar entitled "Headspace" and "Review Goals." If I don't schedule time to do something, it doesn't happen. This is also why I don't have long, exhaustive to-do lists. If it's not important enough to schedule, it's not important.

IF YOU DON'T HAVE IT ON YOUR CALENDAR, IT'S NOT IMPORTANT!

5. **Talk a good game.** After I work out but before I start my workday, I engage in positive self-talk. I tell myself, "You got this, big boy." It's a mantra I've used since my college sports days that helps me stay focused and persist.

The right attitude will never be permanent. It takes conscious daily effort. Wordspeak, chants and positive affirmations are methods that help some people. If you don't buy into positive affirmations or setting goals, at least understand that negative thoughts will bring negative repercussions.

Without a daily process that *mentally* sets you up for success, you are setting yourself up for *real* failure.

WHEN YOUR ENEMY BECOMES YOUR B.F.F.

Gatekeepers suck!

At least that's what I hear from sales reps all the time.

To me, they're just people doing the job they're paid to do. Gatekeepers who let you through easily are terrible at their job. Effective gatekeepers are actually one of my greatest sources of competitive advantage. I'll explain in a minute.

When it comes to gatekeepers, I prepare for the worst. If you think you're going to walk through the door of a new customer and close the sale with ease, you're tricking yourself. If you walk into a new account knowing you very well might not get past the gatekeeper, any small amount of progress after that feels like a win.

What's the trick to getting to a decision maker? There's no trick at all. Persist.

CHECK IT OUT ONLINE According to InsideSales.com, most salespeople make an average of 1.3 phone calls before giving up on a lead.[5] What they don't know is that by calling back that same lead a second, third, fourth or more times, they can double or even triple their chances of closing that sale. Check out the visual on the next page (you can print this out as a reminder of the potential that already exists within your CRM by visiting www.knuckledraggingsales.com/book):

---

5   https://www.insidesales.com/insider/lead-management/lead-response-management-infographic/

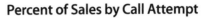

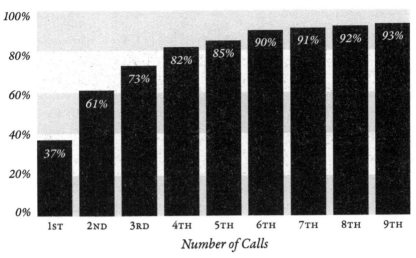

Percent of Sales by Call Attempt

Number of Calls

The next time you complain about the lack of fresh leads, remember that you can nearly *triple* your sales just by calling back the leads you already have! What I like about this statistic is it tells me that all I have to do is make two calls to the same lead and I'm already beating my competition.

This also explains why gatekeepers are assets to Knuckle Draggers. The stronger the gatekeeper, the greater the probability your competitor can't get through either. Gatekeepers keep out sales reps who half-ass it. Be the one who persists and wins.

I look at the gatekeeper like he or she is a potential friend. With persistence, I'll eventually break through. At that point, the gatekeeper becomes my greatest ally, preventing my competition from getting to the buyer at all.

Don't leave a voicemail and consider it a job well done. Don't let a gatekeeper tell you, "Sorry, he's all tied up" and cross that name off your list. Persist!

LONE WOLVES DON'T LIVE LONG

Speaking of allies, there's one group of people you can never do without. It's the people around you. I don't care what job you have—teamwork is essential. Seth Godin coined the term "tribe" to describe any group of people connected to one another through a company, a leader, an idea or virtually anything else. I love that because millions of years ago our ancient ancestors relied heavily on their tribe.

There were no lone wolf cavemen. A lone wolf caveman was just a dead caveman.

As a sales rep, you're more independent than those in other roles. However, working as a teammate makes your job easier.

Inevitably, you'll need help from others—you're not a one-man or one-woman show—so it's vital to learn how to be a team player. Every thriving salesperson I know works well with other people and departments.

I've seen tough-to-deal-with sales reps get pushed down the priority list simply because they couldn't play nice with others. They could have made so much more money if they subscribed to a team mentality.

In my tribe, we live not by the Golden Rule but by the Platinum Rule. The Golden Rule assumes that everyone else is going to respond well to the same words, rewards and incentives that inspire you.

If you think about it, that's pretty selfish. *In contrast, the Platinum Rule says that you should treat others the way* they *want to be treated.* It shifts the focus from you and forces you to understand what makes everyone around you (including your buyers) tick. It's *selfless* rather than selfish.

This is how you create a great team environment.

If given the choice, I'll take a rookie with a great attitude and strong team spirit over a veteran with a poisonous attitude and no desire to contribute to the team. We can accomplish exponentially more together than anyone can ever do alone.

Sales reps are often considered lone wolves. It can be easy to feel alone in the struggle since most of us are in the field by ourselves. But there's a difference between a lone wolf and a good teammate.

I considered myself a lone wolf at one point in my career. Once I learned the business and wasn't relying on other people to teach me, I began operating in a vacuum. I may not have needed to "be taught" anymore, but I eventually realized that being a good team member also means helping others, not just being helped!

Sales is a pendulum. You may be riding the high of closing a big deal and having a great year. Inevitably, it will eventually swing the other way. If you want to learn how to think like a team member, it starts by keeping a positive attitude and not bringing other team members down. If you don't offer help or encouragement to those who need it, who will offer you help when your pendulum swings the other way?

If you've been a good teammate, you'll have lots of people in your corner for support whenever you need it. What about the lone wolf with a bad attitude and an inability to play nice with others? Not so much.

Adding a team dynamic to anything always makes it more complex. That's when attitude becomes more critical than ever. Never allow your bad attitude to become the iceberg that sinks the team's ship. Choose to work with only those who believe that the whole is greater than the sum of its parts.

SORRY, YOU AREN'T THAT SPECIAL

As we wrap up this chapter, let's review some of the most critical pieces of a knuckle-dragging attitude:

1. **Attitude is the constant in all success stories.** Every time I've experienced overwhelming success in my life, there has been one constant—my attitude. During those times, I believed I could overcome any roadblock, and I persisted. My attitude may not have been all sunshine and rainbows, but it was laser focused on why the hell I had gotten out of bed that morning. Fear propelled me to fight, and I didn't allow corrosive thoughts to steal my determination.

2. **Expecting the worst is not a bad attitude; it's a preparation strategy.** I know I will encounter roadblocks. I prepare to not get the appointment or the sale. I prepare to have to call on the same prospect nine times before she'll agree to see me. Those expectations are what set your mind to work and get you thinking about solutions to problems before they even arise!

3. **Your attitude needs a routine.** My day would fall apart without my attitude routine, which starts the night before. My planned workouts, meditations, daily goal reviews and positive affirmations are the vital components my mind needs to get my attitude up to speed every morning.

4. **Gatekeepers don't have to dictate your attitude.** For many sales reps, gatekeepers are the biggest attitude destroyer of all. They'll always be there, and the good ones force you to stay sharp, get creative and most importantly, persist. Persistence is the one and only strategy that works when it comes to gatekeepers.

5. **Maintaining the right attitude is not a solo activity.** When it comes to attitude, why would you take it solely upon yourself to stay positive? If *you* are your only support system, your attitude will eventually falter, and there will be no one to lean on to get it right again. Your team is invaluable. They support, encourage and

help you when your supplies are exhausted. Be a good team member, and you'll feel the love in return!

Even after we've laid out all these pieces, it's possible that you're thinking something similar to, "Yeah, but you don't know what I've been through."

That's true, I don't. You may have had a tough road. You may also think you've had more than your fair share of problems, and all of that stuff has gotten in the way on your path to success. If you can relate to those sentiments, I have some news for you:

You aren't that special. We've *all* got stuff. You're not the only one dealing with health problems, crazy relatives, fussy newborns or relationship troubles.

Shit gets real no matter how carefully you try to avoid distractions, problems, people who suck and predators who try to eat you alive. But if you focus on your why and set up systems and processes to stay focused, you can and will get through it.

We all wish we could steer clear of the mess and cruise through life. But it doesn't work that way. There's nothing you can do about the crap life throws at you.

But *you can* control your attitude and how you spend your time. People who consistently earn seven figure incomes are not partying, watching TV every night, goofing off or bitching about everything that's wrong. They're picking up their clubs, bashing through gatekeepers and selling.

You can also control how much time you spend around attitude destroyers—the seagulls that come in, crap on your picnic and leave. Seagulls love to be critics. In my experience, critics of the sales world are those who are average and want everyone else to stay average with them. When they see you adopt a different attitude, they'll tell you you're wasting your time.

Just smile and keep on persisting—because you and they both know the truth.

If you feel like life has thrown you too many curve balls, there's a cure for what ails you. Persist.

Lack of momentum? Persist.

Can't get in the door? Persist.

Prospect won't give you an answer? Persist.

Rude prospects and gatekeepers? Get over it and persist.

There are no obstacles to your success. There are just excuses why you're not persisting and persevering.

People often ask me what the secret is to success. I always chuckle a little inside when I hear that.

> WHEN YOU ADOPT A KNUCKLE-DRAGGING ATTITUDE, THE WORST-CASE SCENARIO IS THAT IT'S JUST A MATTER OF TIME BEFORE YOU GET THE SALE.

It's not a secret! It's the right attitude.

Just keep fighting! You will get knocked down. Get back up.

You will be told no. Ask the question a different way.

You will be treated like a piece of garbage. Smile and try again.

The Knuckle Draggers of days gone by had real problems. They worried about being eaten by saber-toothed tigers. They died from cholera and dysentery. They didn't have toilet paper. Let that sink in for a minute. How miserable would you be if you didn't have TP? Those are legit problems.

A legit problem is *not* only getting one week's paid vacation between Christmas and New Year's!

What I love about sales is that being successful and making a *ton* of money requires *zero* talent. It's about persistence. It's about dogged determination. Just keep fighting! That's the Knuckle Dragger mentality.

Knuckle Draggers don't complain about gatekeepers. They crush the gatekeeper's skull with a wooden club (metaphorically speaking) and close the sale. The knuckle-dragging mentality is about knowing you'll get the sale regardless of inevitable obstacles.

"Goals are meaningless
words on paper until you
reverse engineer them to be targeted,
intentional and attainable."

John Crowley

CHAPTER FOUR

THE CAVEMAN'S GUIDE TO GOAL SETTING

I am not here to try and replace your "thing" if your thing is working for you. Maybe you've been telling yourself you're working so you can sail away on a yacht one day. You even have photos of that dream yacht on your bathroom mirror. If that pumps you up to go sell day after day, great!

Maybe your why is your family, and looking at their smiling faces on your phone is all it takes for you to keep fighting. If that's the case, then you know what they say about stuff that ain't broke.

But let me ask you this: if your why is a person, thing or feeling and you're still living paycheck to paycheck, could it be that you haven't honed in on what truly propels you?

And could it be that you're only setting goals so you can tell people you have goals?

That's why we spent the first few chapters getting our minds right and retraining our focus. Before you can *do*, you have to *believe you can*.

You also have to find a why that inspires action. Here's my why: I fear life without money and what having no money would mean to my future and family. It's a powerful and a lasting motivator.

Once you know your why, you have to make an intense and constant effort to get your mind right and persist. Once you have this resolve in place, it's on to the next step: setting aggressive but attainable goals.

LET'S GET SIMPLE

Before we go any further, let's call this chapter what it really is: Goal Setting for Dummies. Don't get offended. I'm not calling you a dummy— the dummy is me.

I may not be the sharpest tool in the shed, but I learned a long time ago that reading books and studying the mindsets, habits and actions of other successful people leads to success. I've spent the better part of the last decade reading (okay, listening to) every book about business, success and sales I could find.

Ironically, the more I read, the more I discovered how simple success in sales can be. I've learned that simple is better *and* pays better.

Whenever I find that something isn't working, I poke around to figure out why. I almost always find that I've taken something that should have been straightforward and made it needlessly complicated.

The cavemen didn't have time to overthink anything. There were no "hunting seminars" or "gathering symposiums." They just went out and did what they had to do.

Don't get me wrong—modern life is great. I'm not interested in reverting back to a time of loincloths and drawing on walls.

But I do respect the simplicity of their existence. There weren't cavemen motivational speakers or primitive trainers telling them they've been sharpening their spears all wrong. They learned through experience.

And they either learned the lesson or died.

Harsh—yes. Simple—also yes.

The same goes for goal setting.

When I first started setting goals, I tried to keep them simple. The problem was that my goals weren't specific enough to compel action or to drive the right activity.

I had confused *simple* with *generic*.

Then I made goal setting too complicated. My list was a mile long and filled with minu-

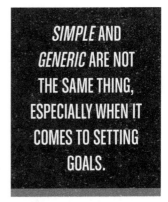

SIMPLE AND *GENERIC* ARE NOT THE SAME THING, ESPECIALLY WHEN IT COMES TO SETTING GOALS.

tiae. I'd open up the list in the morning and feel paralyzed by the magnitude of it all.

Next, I prioritized my list by order of importance. By the end of the year, I'd done a lot, but it hadn't advanced my goals. I was basically a human hamster, putting a lot of effort into running on a wheel that wasn't taking me anywhere.

These days, I believe less is more. I have a single spreadsheet of my goals for the year, and I work on one goal per day.

I took a goal-setting course last year that claimed the magic number of goals is between seven and nine. Any less than seven goals and you aren't pushing yourself. During the course, I set goals for all parts of my life—including my health, relationships, personal development, finances and career.

When I finished the course, I had six goals that were supported by dozens of tasks. But back at home, as I went through my morning ritual and reviewed my goals, I was flooded with anxiety. I had created a to-do list so detailed that I would need to quit my job and neglect my family if I wanted to accomplish everything on it. I was so overwhelmed that I suffered from goal paralysis.

So I returned to my knuckle-dragging roots. I simplified. I decided that completing this book was the most important goal. The book would help me land speaking gigs and serve as the framework for our coaching program. It would also become the syllabus for the collegiate sales class I dream of teaching and would give instant credibility to my consulting business. It would be part of my legacy.

If you struggle with setting, sticking to and accomplishing goals, try the knuckle-dragging method. Start with one goal. Identify the outcome that, when accomplished, will serve as a springboard for all future goals.

And now for the million-dollar question: *How do you take an abstract goal and monetize it through targeted activity?*

It's not easy. I'm still figuring it out. But along the way, I've made some great strides. Notice that not every goal needs to be about money. But every goal needs to contribute to your BHAG. I'll explain it by walking you through my own goals for 2018. Take a look at the spreadsheet on the following page. There are seven major aspects:

1. Goal and Deadline

This one should be pretty obvious. This is the *short* list of things you want to accomplish. And your deadlines should be fairly aggressive. Otherwise, it becomes this nebulous thing that gets backburnered into obscurity.

2. Referee

I need help. I like help. So I have referees for each of my goals. I used to be a lone wolf, but when I decided to be a wolf who also relies heavily on his pack, my bank account and happiness level grew.

The best referees are subject matter experts. Ideally, they're paid mentors and coaches rather than close friends or a spouse. A paid coach motivates you in ways no one else can. The right

2018 GOALS
BHAG: $10M liquid by age 50

GOAL	DEADLINE	REFEREE	CARROT/STICK	HOW	STATUS	WHY	Jan	Feb	Mar	Apr	May	Jun	Jul	Aug	Sep	Oct	Nov	Dec
Lose 20 lbs	3/1/2018	Jeb	Carrot: Bi-monthly massages	Purchase & implement intermittent fasting program Lift: Mon, Wed, Fri Yoga: Tue, Thu, Sun	Complete	Confidence and improved sleep	■	■	■									
Publish Knuckle Dragging Sales	5/1/2018	Jen Lill	Carrot: North Carolina Red Drum fishing trip	Hire designer for book and logo Set up Create-Space for Amazon Build website Create Launch Team Record audiobook	On-track	Credibility and frame-work for coaching program	■	■	■	■	■							
Sign 10 paid coaching clients	9/1/2018	Jen Lill	Stick: No fall break vacation	Launch Team Pilot Create & test coaching program LinkedIn advertising course	Not started	THIS IS WHAT YOU LOVE! You cannot hit your BHAG just working in corporate America						■	■	■	■			
Book 5 paid speaking gigs	12/31/2018	Baldwin	Stick: No winter break vacation	Create KDS keynote Join Nashville Toastmasters "Book & Paid to Speak" Elite course	Not started	THIS IS WHAT YOU LOVE! Coaching lead gen										■	■	■

coach will hold you accountable to your goals. Having some money riding on the outcome also helps propel action.

3. Carrot/Stick

I use rewards and penalties to keep me on track with my goals. If I hit the goal, I reward myself (the carrot). I don't, I face repercussions (the stick). Are you struggling to hit your fitness goals? Take an embarrassing picture of yourself in a bathing suit, send it to your referee, and instruct her to post it on Facebook if you miss your weight loss goal. If you're like me, you'll find that the stick is mightier than the carrot.

4. How (Reverse Engineer)

This simple column represents what used to be a ridiculously long and complicated to-do list. Breaking down each goal into the tiniest activities is exhausting. The "how" takes your abstract goal and starts giving you the steps needed to get there. Remember to keep it simple.

For example, I knew it would take a lot of steps to write this book. But on my spreadsheet, I simplified the process. Every small step I took fell under the umbrella of one of the steps on my spreadsheet.

When I'm consulting, one of the most common mistakes I see clients make is not using *reverse engineering* when setting goals. Here's how to utilize reverse engineering to set targets that are actually attainable. First, figure out your Big Hairy Audacious Goal (BHAG), a lofty goal with a long-term (multiple year) deadline. Next, break it down piece-by-piece, starting from the end and working backwards. Along the way, you'll figure out what tactics will get you to the final destination.

REVERSE ENGINEERING IS THE KEY TO MONETIZING GOALS.

For example, start-ups love to set ambitious goals like, "Make $100,000 in monthly revenue."

A statement like that requires that you know how much each customer is worth. Hell, it requires that you know how much each conversation is worth! It entails research, documentation and discussions of ROI and other scary three-letter finance acronyms.

My next question for them is, "Okay, do you have the necessary infrastructure, products and/or customers to make that amount each month?"

They respond with, "Well, if I sell my $100 widget to each customer, I'll need 1,000 customers to make $100,000 in sales."

My next question is, "Do you have access to 1,000 potential customers each month?"

"No."

I keep spoon-feeding them. "Then what do you have to do?"

"Um, increase the price per customer?"

Bingo!

That's how you use reverse engineering to find the tactics for making your goal a reality.

5. Status

This part is my yardstick. Have I done it yet? Putting an X in this column gives me that satisfying feeling of triumph. It makes all those "You got this, big boy" pep talks, morning gym sessions and working weekends worth it. This column is also a great way to gauge my overall progress. If I don't start seeing Xs in those squares as the year goes on, it means I need to seriously rethink my "how" lists. I may also need to go back to the goals themselves. Were they too aggressive? Did I attempt too many goals in one year? A lack of Xs means something is wrong, and it may take some recalculating to figure out what is not working and why.

6. Why

My big why is the fear of not having the money I need to support my family and leave a kick-ass legacy for my girls. But each goal also has its own motivators. For example, my weight loss goal is partially money-driven (being in shape gives me more energy, which makes me better at my job, which helps me earn more money). But I also want to feel better, look better and avoid preventable disease, all of which will make me happier and help me be a better husband, father and friend.

7. Focus Times

I came up with this grid out of necessity. Whether you have 60 goals or six, it's impossible to focus on all of them at once. If you try to tackle them all at once, I guarantee you'll be half-assing most of them. This grid calendar allows me to visualize the times during the year when I'll be in hot pursuit of a certain goal. This means that other goals on the list won't get much attention during that time. And that's okay. They'll have their moment in the sun.

At the beginning of every day, an appointment goes on my calendar. That appointment is an activity that supports one of my goals. Working out every morning addresses my health goal. So at the very least, if I accomplish nothing else that day in direct pursuit of a goal, I can go to bed knowing that I engaged in one activity that moved the ball forward.

More than anything else, goal setting and goal tracking are skills that must be practiced. If you've never goal hunted, you're probably going to suck at it. But I'm fairly certain that no fledgling hunter millions of years ago snagged a woolly mammoth with his first spear.

CHECK IT OUT ONLINE Big victories take time and practice to achieve. Trust me—it's worth it. You'll feel victorious when you become adept at setting worthwhile, attainable goals that stimulate profit-producing action. Go to www.knuckledraggingsales.com/book to download your own goal tracking spreadsheet template.

If you start tracking your goals and discover it comes easy to you, congratulations—you are officially a goal-setting prodigy. For the rest of us, just stick with it and keep adjusting as you go along. The most important thing is to persist!

THE LEAST HELPFUL ADVICE EVER

One of my pet peeves in life is successful people's use of the word "lucky." It really drives me crazy.

One of the success "hacks" (also hate that word) I regularly read about is finding someone who has already done what you're trying to accomplish and asking how they did it. Advisors and success coaches say things like, "Don't reinvent the wheel. Avoid mistakes by asking successful, wealthy people who already made those mistakes how to avoid them."

Sounds great! Except that when I've asked those folks what they did to get to where they are today, they get all humble on me.

"Oh, I just got lucky."

Now, I get it—I really do. Nobody wants to sound like a pompous jerk by patting himself on the back for all his hard work and right actions.

But here's the thing. The "lucky" response is not helpful.

Should you bother asking? Yes! Just be prepared to dig and possibly pay them for their time and expertise.

If you're talking to someone who has the things you want (career, money, etc.), don't let him or her get away with, "I got lucky." Ask specific questions. Peel back the onion. Get even the faintest glimpse of the harrowing and exhausting work it took for them to get where they are.

I guarantee you that these successful people had big goals that helped them reach such high levels of achievement. It wasn't by accident.

People with goals are intentional. It's been proven. According to a 2015 study conducted by Dr. Gail Matthews, a psychology professor at Dominican University in California, you are 42 percent more likely to achieve your goals just by writing them down.[6]

I would be remiss if I didn't mention one other key ingredient of the goal pie. A group of scientists affiliated with Brown University, UC Berkeley and the National Institutes of Health conducted a study to determine the key factor in alcoholics' ability to get sober. The answer was both simple and surprising:

Belief.

According to the report, "Belief was the key ingredient that made a reworked habit (staying sober) loop into a permanent behavior."[7]

Believe—and if you don't believe you can do it, then don't write it down. If you write down a goal that's so unrealistic you doubt you can do it, you need one of two things: a new goal or some mental tough love.

Like having the right attitude, pursuing goals is a constant battle that must be fought every single day. And after you win (aka reach a goal), guess what? There's no down time. You need to get back into the arena and fight to reach the next goal.

Again it comes back to that fighter's spirit. Do you have the fight in you or not?

I'm not sure there's a foolproof goal setting system that works for everyone. I had to create my own because I could never find the right fit

6   Hyatt, Michael. "Five Reasons Why You Should Commit Your Goals to Writing." Michaelhyatt.com. Retrieved from https://michaelhyatt.com/5-reasons-why-you-should-commit-your-goals-to-writing.html.

7   Duhigg, Charles. *The Power of Habit: Why We Do What We Do in Life and Business.* N.p.: Random House, 2012. Print.

for me. After reading lots of books on goal setting and attending plenty of courses, seminars and workshops, I've come up with my own primitive goal setting method. It works for me.

Maybe it will work for you, too. But for it to be effective, it takes conscious effort, daily focus and *lots* of knuckle-dragging simplification.

"Little fish don't
win you big trophies."

John Crowley

CHAPTER FIVE

BIG FISH

I recently read an article about an interesting and popular dictum in the health and fitness industry:

"Complicate to profit."

This motto refers to how fitness business giants intentionally complicate things to convince people they need to buy a particular product, piece of equipment or program.

For example, they work hard to convince would-be bodybuilders that they need a line of scientifically formulated products, taken at the exact same time every day for a required number of weeks or months, along with a specific diet and exercise program. Failure to adhere to this rigorous and product-intensive schedule will result in disappointing outcomes.

Most fitness enthusiasts say that it is only by simplifying the complex that they're able to stick to a plan and reach their fitness goals. The key to being fit and strong is simple: eat clean and exercise more. Want bigger muscles? Lift more. Need endurance? Run. Want to lose weight? Eat real food and move more.

That's about as complicated as it needs to get. Yet fitness companies have taken all that beautiful simplicity and muddied the waters. They've turned the words "health and fitness" into an intimidating multi-billion-dollar industry.

Why do they do it? Because if you over-complicate something that is simple, people tend to buy into the hype in order to gain the perceived reward. Unfortunately, that's also exactly what's happened in sales. "Sales gurus" earn big bucks by complicating simple ideas.

"You need this training, followed by that training, followed by one-on-one coaching, followed by this software and that software."

They try to convince us that the path to success is complicated—and that they have all the answers. But if we pay them the low price of $499 a month for a year, we can have the answers, too.

I don't blame them for wanting you to think there's no silver bullet. If you realized how simple the answer really was, you wouldn't need them at all.

We buy the lie that all the "stuff" is going to get us where we need to be. Spend enough money on the right programs, software, coaching and books, and you can buy success! No actual work required.

What they neglect to tell you is that none of the stuff works if you don't commit to putting in the real work of being a salesperson—and that the work will only yield results if you (wait for it) *persist!*

These sales "experts" are complicating to profit, but in order to crush quota, we simplify. And so the dictum becomes:

"They may complicate to profit, but we simplify to grow."

Let me pause my rant and say that I get it. It's so easy to get overwhelmed with acquiring, using and doing all the stuff of life.

Stuff clouds our schedule every day. You can fill an eight-hour day with email alone. And then there's social media, which is both the greatest modern tool for salespeople and the most potent productivity destroyer in the history of business.

Stuff = anything that doesn't directly move a sale forward with one of your biggest potential customers (your Big Fish). The reason it's called stuff is because it fills voids in your day. It also gives the false illusion of accomplishment.

Think about the stuffing inside a turkey. The stuffing is a great complement to the real meat of the meal. But it's supposed to be a side dish to the main entrée, not a replacement for the meat itself!

This stuff has really screwed with our business. It doesn't have to anymore. No more days filled with all the stuff that's keeping you broke. In this chapter, we'll discuss the final foundation you need to have in place that will enable you to wake up and perform with efficiency and precision every single day.

In caveman's terms, what we'll do in this chapter is draw pictures of our greatest food sources on the wall. We'll identify the saber-toothed tigers, giant sloths and woolly mammoths. We'll bypass the rodents and baby dodos. They aren't worth your time. You've got mouths to feed.

HOW TO PICK YOUR BIGGEST FISH

Did you know that before the Industrial Revolution, the word "priorities" (with an *s*) didn't exist? There was just "priority"—i.e. the most important thing (with no *s*) you had to do in a day. After the Industrial Revolution, managers realized that they could get more out of people if they gave them more than one priority.

> THERE'S NO SUCH THING AS "PRIORITIES." THERE'S THE MOST IMPORTANT THING AND THEN THERE'S EVERYTHING ELSE.

We've now evolved into a society where people have dozens of priorities.

And they're all of equal importance.

That makes no sense. Yet we live it every day! We prioritize one item of minutia over another. In the end, we have a list of 167 things that all need to be done . . . today.

Is organizing your emails so that you can send out marketing spam *really* as important as closing business in your pipeline? Is printing labels for your new filing system *really* as important as calling on new prospects?

I mean, really?

The *adequate* managers of the world set priorities and then slowly pile on "other stuff" in the form of logging calls, cleaning up CRMs, completing business reviews and doing sales reports (lots and lots of sales reports).

On the other hand, *excellent* leaders set priorities and keep other "stuff" off their sales reps' plates. They recognize that keeping the sales force focused on their Big Fish is the most effective way to hit quota.

If your sales manager prioritizes "stuff" over real, tangible sales activity that leads to more business, that ultimately puts a hard limit on the number of zeros in your bank account.

So what can you do?

First and foremost, you need to find your Big Fish (don't worry, I'll show you how). Then tell your leader your plan to focus on the activities that will most effectively lead to more sales.

It's essential to get permission to structure your day and your activities accordingly. With thoughtful communication, few leaders will reject your plan. It makes too much sense to deny.

Step 1: Separate the qualified leads from the rest.

The first step in the plan is to separate the real from the imaginary. Not every name in your CRM will be a customer. If you're fortunate enough to work for a company with a lead qualifying mechanism or an amazing marketing department, feel grateful. And if you have a mature territory with existing relationships, count your lucky stars.

Also know that you are the exception and not the rule.

Most sales reps have what they feel is the absolute "worst territory." It's too saturated, it's too small, it's too large—it's whatever. Regardless of what you've got to work with, one truth remains:

Unqualified leads = pipeline killers.

If you don't have a qualified lead engine or another efficient way to separate the potential heroes from the zeros, know what your pipeline killers are and ask identifying questions early in the discovery process.

In my business, some of the most common issues that turn a lead into garbage are customers with credit problems, prospects who have signed long-term exclusive deals and practices that have incumbent and integrated technologies (EMRs, or Electronic Medical Records).

Here are some questions I ask to qualify leads before I waste my valuable time:

- **"What are your terms with your current distributor?"** If their answer is more than 30 days, this is a sign they may have trouble paying their bills. I'm not interested in customers who will result in no commission.

- **"Will there be any surprises when we go through a credit check?"** I know this question sounds personal, but I only ask it if I'm comfortable with the prospect. I let them know that we have a stringent credit approval process, so it's important for them to let me know if there's anything in their credit history that might raise red flags.

- **"Are you under any exclusive distribution agreements that would prevent you from switching your business next quarter?"** If they can't switch to us within the next few months, that's not an active lead, plain and simple. It should be taken out of the pile and filed under "revisit in a few months."

- **"If I could give you everything you dreamed of, how quickly could you switch your business?"** This is a great question because it identifies other competing priorities the customer may have that could delay the switch.

These questions might not fit with what you're selling. The point isn't to provide you with every question you need to ask to qualify a lead. The goal is to help you understand the *types* of questions that help you avoid the heartache of wasting weeks or months on a prospect who will never become a customer.

If you don't have qualified leads, this is your first priority. *Sit down and figure out what deal breakers most often lead to dead ends in your business.* Then brainstorm ways to identify those disqualifiers in conversations with prospects.

If possible, try to qualify leads over the phone rather than face-to-face. While not always doable, it certainly saves time when you can do some of the work without leaving your desk.

Step 2: Sort qualified leads by volume.

After you've identified the solid leads from the rest, sort qualified customers by potential volume. This will most likely (and hopefully) be the same metric used to measure your quota.

In my business, we look at annual drug expenditure. This is the total amount of money my customers spend on oncology drugs in a year.

Find out how your company quantifies potential customer size and use that metric for sorting. In healthcare sales, it could be the number of MDs or providers in a practice, number of hospital beds, number of prescriptions, number of patients or another metric.

This step enables you to objectively rank your customers. Now you know who represents the most potential. We're talking about real, tangible potential, not the pie in the sky "wish list" of big customers who may or may not even be qualified.

Step 3: Identify your target number.

After you've sorted your list of qualified leads by potential volume, multiply your quota by three. This is your Big Fish target.

For example, if my quota is $100 million in new business for the year, that means I need to identify $300 million in Big Fish business.

If you work in a finely-tuned sales machine, you can multiply your quota by your close ratio to come up with a more accurate number. Anecdotally, though, I have found that *most sales reps will close one out of every three qualified leads.* This allows for fall-off and other factors you may not have accounted for that turn qualified leads into dead ends.

Step 4: Pick 10 leads that total your target number.

Once you have your target, pick 10 customers whose total business equals that Big Fish target number. In the example above, that would mean I need 10 prospects that represent $300 million in new business if I closed them all. Because I've accounted for a 33 percent close ratio, I can lose two out of three deals and still hit my $100 million quota.

You will cater to these 10 Big Fish over the next year. They'll be the first customers you visit, call and email each week. When you wake up in the morning and plan your day, they'll fill your calendar and preoccupy your mind. After you've engaged in at least one daily activity that keeps the momentum going and reels one or more Big Fish closer to the boat, only then should you work on other "stuff."

Every time you close a Big Fish or the prospect falls off the line, go back to your list of potentials and choose another fish of similar size to take its place.

CHECK IT OUT ONLINE

And so the process goes, until the end of time.

Go to www.knuckledraggingsales.com/book to download a free copy of our Big Fish Worksheet that walks you through these first four steps.

Step 5: Develop a plan to land your Big Fish.

Now you know what Big Fish are all about. But now you may be thinking, "Okay, I've got the boat in the water and I'm ready to fish. What do I use for bait?"

It's all well and good to identify a few big potential customers, but if you don't have the right bait and tackle to reel them in, it doesn't really matter that they're qualified.

Last year, I went fishing with a buddy. When I took out my lure, he belly laughed at me. My hook was huge, while the one he was using was a normal-sized hook. "There's nothing in this river big enough to swallow that hook!"

By the end of the day, my friend had caught half a dozen tiny fish.

I'd caught just one—but it was gigantic.

Nobody cares about the little fish. It's the trophy fish people remember. The same applies to sales. You can expend a bunch of energy fishing for little customers, but they don't win sales contests . . . Big Fish do!

Our De-Evolution Revolution is now well under way. You've gotten a crash course on the foundations that enable you to do the real work of a knuckle-dragging sales professional. Now you'll learn the execution (i.e. the right bait) for reeling in the Big Fish.

We aren't talking about frenzied activity. We're talking about setting big hooks and casting them in the right places to catch the biggest fish.

One of the foundations of survival training is to conserve calories by only engaging in activities that are necessary to sustain life. The cavemen knew this well. If it wasn't going to benefit their tribe, they didn't do it. *Every excursion had a purpose.*

We need to take a lesson from that in order to avoid the burnout that is so widespread in sales. Traditional sales reps who go "dialing for dollars" day in and day out, they just don't last. What's worse is that kind of frantic, non-stop sales activity will eventually lead to the extinction of the sales profession as we know it.

Let's not go the way of the dodo. Avoid career extinction by fighting smart *and* hard, and plan your day accordingly.

Eventually I was able to stop cold calling altogether and get to decision makers who were not just *willing* to meet with me, but who were *excited* at the prospect of working together.

That can be a reality for you, too. So stay with me—the best is yet to come.

PART II:

EXECUTION

"The only thing you have that your competitor doesn't have is *you*. Be different—be someone worthy of being remembered."

John Crowley

CHAPTER SIX

DIFFERENT IS BETTER THAN BETTER

Welcome to Part II! In case you haven't figured it out yet, this book is for people who want to make a lot of money.

When I'm giving a keynote or training at a company and I tell the audience that they can make seven figures in selling, jaws drop. After that initial reaction, I usually see one of two expressions radiating from people's faces: They either don't believe me, or they get excited.

I've written this book for those of you who get excited when someone says, "Here's how you make seven figures without ever going back to school, without ever becoming a crooked politician, without years of medical training. You don't even have to have letters like CEO or CFO on your business card."

I've also written this book for people who understand that the greatest rewards in life are earned by those who DO. THE. WORK. There are no handouts. There is no easy money. The cavemen who survived and had big families were the ones who did what was necessary, and did it so often that they became experts.

Kids may never aspire to be us on career day, but they should. Why? Because genuine, bonafide knuckle-dragging salespeople are wealthy. They put in the time and persist even when they don't feel like it.

They may also feel like quitting. But they don't. And they eventually win.

What do they win? The security and freedom that can only come from having a big bank account.

So here we go.

WE CAN'T ALL SELL VIAGRA

There are a lot of great salespeople. There are a lot of great products. That means the only way to stand out is to be better than the rest, right?

Or maybe the answer is to have the best product?

Okay, the best price?

I know! Just work harder than everyone else.

The only real way to get ahead is exactly none of those things.

In the battle for top sales rep status and seven figure incomes, *different* is *so* much better than *better*.

The strongest product asset you could ever have is uniqueness. I'm not talking about the uniqueness of your widget or service. I'm talking about you. You are the product.

If you don't see yourself as the product, then you're going to completely disappear in a sea of other salespeople who are selling similar (maybe even identical) stuff. You'll be doomed to obscurity. And I know about obscurity.

Before I was a Healthcare Sales Mentor, I began my career in pharmaceutical sales in the cushiest, easiest and most fortunate way possible. One of my first product launches at Pfizer was Viagra—the one product that literally anyone could sell.

"It's a pill that does *what?*"

My sales day consisted of having the red carpet rolled out because every doctor, nurse, receptionist and secretary wanted Viagra samples. Grandmothers would stop me in the lobby of office buildings begging for samples (or begging me not to give samples to their husbands). Viagra was a currency accepted everywhere by everyone.

Here's the problem: Viagra sold itself. The infomercials and press releases drummed up so much interest that I didn't even need to talk about the product. Patients and doctors demanded it.

I'm not complaining about the Viagra launch. It was *awesome!* I was 25 years old and was making more money than I ever imagined. The problem was the Viagra launch became my benchmark. All launches were easy . . . right?

Wrong!

My next new product was typical of the standard product launch. It was a "me-too" drug with no compelling benefits, a boring birth control pill.

There were plenty of birth control pills already on the market. And they were all 99 percent effective. Boring. To make matters more boring, most physicians were comfortable with the incumbent product. Not only were doctors uninterested in switching products, but there was nothing compelling about my product that I could use to convince them.

In other words, I had to sell.

This sales thing is hard!

For a year, I spun my wheels. I made twice as many calls as my peers. I called on every last potential customer, big and small (I hadn't figured out Big Fish yet). I closed and closed hard.

"Doctor, will you put your next ten patients on my drug?"

(I'm embarrassed just thinking about it.)

One day I met a stunning blonde colleague who gave me some of the best advice of my career. She said, "You're working too hard, stupid."

It was such compelling advice that I later married that blonde. My soon-to-be wife explained that when all else is equal, people buy from people they know, like and trust.

I realized that I needed to persist, but at the same time, I had to change the perception that I was just another pushy rep.

Was that possible? I wasn't sure yet, but I did know that doctors appreciated sales reps who respected their busy schedules. They also didn't want to be pressured. Okay, so what could I do with this boring, me-too drug? My product was far from novel. That meant it was up to *me*.

I needed to be different from the competition.

I thought about what made me unique. What makes John Crowley memorable? I started with the most obvious thing, which is that I'm a *gigantic* ginger. For anyone who doesn't know, "gingers" are those of us who have been blessed with fire red hair, pale skin that blisters in the sun, and freckles . . . so many freckles.

I bought a case of Big Red gum at Costco and affixed stickers to every pack that said, "Compliments of John Crowley, your *Big Red* head Pfizer rep."

Corny—yep.

Embarrassing—you know it.

Effective—hell yes.

I replaced the practice of stalking physicians during busy office hours with leaving my Big Red gum calling card. When doctors saw a pile of Big Red gum, they knew I had been there and had elected not to bother them.

They came to appreciate my empathy for their hectic schedules and large patient load. Eventually, something really cool happened. When I did pop in unannounced and they weren't busy, they would invite me in for a conversation.

They loved the Big Red gimmick. As cheesy and self-deprecating as it was, it worked because I was different.

Doctors' perceptions of sales reps are the same—pretty faces, nice suits and product knowledge that's about an inch wide and a mile deep. In their eyes, sales reps can talk to you for hours about their *one* product, and that's it.

I had differentiated myself from an endless sea of cookie cutter sales reps. More importantly, I was memorable. How could you not smile at a gigantic ginger who was willing to poke fun at one of his biggest insecurities?

I was starting to see how being *different* really was better than being *better*.

UNLIKELY HOBBY, BIG REVELATION

What is one hobby you'd never expect to see a big, hulking, redheaded guy enjoying? Sun bathing? Maybe horse jockey?

I just so happen to be the world's largest yoga instructor. I went through 200 hours of training to become a yogi. The end result was a 240-pound ginger bending in ways that would make most gymnasts jealous.

One of the mantras that my yoga teacher always used stuck with me: *Imitate, integrate and innovate.* When I first heard it, I thought, "Wow, that's exactly how to become really great in sales."

The easiest way to pick up a new skill is by observing those who are successful and *imitating* the actions that made them successful. *Integrating* those tactics into your own routine is the fastest way to success. Once you've mastered those tactics, it's time to *innovate*.

I can hear you now. "But I thought you said to be different and *not* copy the competition."

That's true. If you copy your competition indefinitely, you'll find yourself at the bottom of the sales heap and probably broke. However, when you're starting out in sales, the fastest way to learn is to imitate.

Here's how the *imitate, integrate, innovate* path looked for my sales career:

During my first year, I *imitated* the best sales reps. I didn't want to start from scratch and act like I was the first guy to ever call on a doctor. Plenty of successful people have done it every day for years. So I watched and learned.

By my second year, I was able to fully *integrate* the most effective techniques into my sales process. I took what I had learned from the best in the industry and combined the actions, techniques and mind-sets to create a near-seamless process for everything I encountered on a daily basis.

In year three, I began to *innovate*. I constantly tried new techniques to see what worked with my personality and my customers. Some bombed! Others resonated with my customers and became habits. The really good methods are what we're going to talk about in the remainder of this book.

How do you find your differentiator? It's a personal journey. The only one who can decide "What makes me unique?" is you.

You don't have to use a gimmick to stand out. It helps, but there are other ways. Before we get to those, let's briefly cover the mindsets that are key to being different.

1. Be Brave

First, you must be brave. Copying your competition is safe and holds no risk of rejection. That's okay in the beginning when you're learning the business. However, to make real money, you have to innovate.

Sticking your "innovation neck" out there requires bravery. Being brave and being a fighter go hand in hand. If you've already determined that you're a fighter, dig a little deeper and resolve to also be brave. You'll unquestionably need that trait in order to stand out.

2. Be a Listener (a Real One)

The most effective innovators listen to their customers. What does the customer value? What is important to the customer? How can you align your brand with what's important to your perspective buyer?

There's a difference between *pretending to listen* and *actually listening*. When you rely heavily on canned scripts and elevator pitches to do all your selling for you, something happens. You may look like you're listening, but you'll be so busy waiting for an opportunity to talk that you won't hear a word the other person says.

When I listened, I heard from doctors that they hated salespeople who disrupted their day. When I caught physicians between appointments, I annoyed them, inconvenienced their patients and ticked off the office staff who had to stay late so the doctor could finish his or her day.

Don't get me wrong—the "show up and throw up" tactic that most pharmaceutical manufacturers teach does work. Sales reps barge in and spout their factsheet-style presentations into as many faces as possible because that's what they're taught to do.

Knock on *enough* doors and eventually you'll find *enough* prospects willing to put up with your long-winded, annoying pitch.

But it doesn't add value to your customer! It doesn't create partnerships or foster long-term relationships. It's self-serving. You may make the sale today, but at what expense tomorrow?

3. Be Empathetic

By thinking about the customer and *their* customers (the patients) first, I built credibility as a customer-friendly sales professional. While empathy is not a character trait synonymous with salespeople, it's one that leaves a lasting impression with buyers because they so rarely experience it.

I think most of us can agree that there are plenty of good people out there. There's the guy who lets you into his lane during rush hour. There's the waitress who comps your kid some ice cream. But no one expects much out of salespeople.

Be the exception. Be a listener. Be empathic. Be brave. Be different.

I remember how uneasy I felt the first time I left a pack of Big Red behind. What if they laughed at me? What if the nurses thought I was a total tool? Eventually, my competition would see it. Would they use it to sell against me?

Initially, I was pretty wrapped up in the awareness that I could come across as an idiot. But I knew something had to change, and it wasn't going to be my product.

I had to change their perception of *me*.

That's when I resolved to think, "Look, I don't know how this gimmick will be received, but I *do* know it's different. And that's gotta count for something."

I knew I'd struck a nerve the day I noticed that my competitor had started leaving boxes of candy with a sticker that read, "From Bob, Your Ortho Rep."

Eventually, Bob quit leaving candy boxes because he was copying me. He was a hack. A fraud. Everybody knew Big Red was the original.

HOW TO BE DIFFERENT IN A SEA OF "MEH"

If you Google "how to stand out in sales," you'll see a lot of general advice. Some of it's good. Some of it's ridiculous. I see "be yourself" frequently listed. I also see "add value" and "don't bad-mouth the competition" a lot.

That's all good advice. But no amount of sales instruction will do you any good if you can't even get in front of your buyer.

A 2012 *Harvard Business Review* study found that 90 percent of executives (VP and above) *never* respond to cold emails or phone calls.[8] That was 2012. The level of sales activity has only been amplified in the years since. I'd suspect executive responsiveness has only decreased.

How do most sales leaders respond to underperformance? They demand that their sales team make *more* calls. They believe that if you

---

8   https://hbr.org/2012/07/tweet-me-friend-me-make-me-buy

throw more hooks in the water, you increase your chances of catching a fish.

Sorry, but this technique doesn't increase the number of fish. It only increases the fish's exposure to hooks. Over time, the fish become accustomed to the hooks.

Eventually, they completely ignore the hooks.

"Look, everybody! Another hook. Just what we need."

That's what happens when you blast your prospects with emails. First they ignore your lazy attempt to get their attention. After a while, they get annoyed. Eventually, you piss them off.

Rather than being forgotten, you become despised.

The definition of *lunacy* is repeating the same thing and expecting different results. The act of making more calls or sending more emails after the first few rounds of unsuccessful calls and emails is *lunacy!* If you want different results, you must act differently.

I know that seeing a phrase like "how to be different" may lead some to doubt how unique these ideas could be. Let me put your mind at ease. They *are* unique, and here's why:

Most people do the bare minimum to not get fired. The odds are really good that you'll be the only person within a few hundred square miles using tactics that require conscious effort and a little extra exertion.

The major issues plaguing the sales industry result from the "do just enough" mentality that is running amok in our country.

The salespeople who get into sales thinking it will be easy and are shocked when it turns out to be hard are the reason why we hate salespeople!

It's not the people who turn their jobs into long, lucrative careers who we can't stomach—it's those salespeople who are a few months from quitting because they don't have the will, the fight, the energy or the work ethic to last.

Be unique in your approach and it will go a long way. Here are my three favorite ways to stand out from the competition and grab the attention of your potential buyer:

1. Write a Note

As a pharmaceutical sales rep, I spent *a lot* of time waiting to catch physicians. I'd dream about delivering my stunning and highly effective ten-second elevator pitch if I were ever given the chance to use it. I envisioned stopping the hurrying doctor between patients and inspiring her to use my product with an attention-grabbing opener.

The reality was that I looked like a robot, trained by pharmaceutical giants to regurgitate canned openers that marketers believed would inspire physicians to prescribe my drug.

That all changed one day when I sat in an office waiting to snare a physician. The mailman—who afforded more value delivering mail than I did dropping off drug samples—handed the receptionist a mound of mail.

I quietly observed the receptionist make quick work of sorting the "keepers" from the "junk." She discarded several glossy brochures sent by pharmaceutical companies (much like the ones I clutched in my sweaty palms). All that remained from the pile of solicitations were a few bills and what appeared to be a birthday card.

That was my eureka moment.

To get attention, I needed to be different from all the other garbage that came across their desk. I immediately left the office, went to the office supply store and purchased a stack of notecards.

CHECK IT OUT ONLINE

Handwritten notes are a true rarity today—the double rainbow of communication (check out double rainbow guy at www.knuckledraggingsales.com/book).

According to a 2011 U.S. Postal Service survey, the average home received a personal letter once every seven weeks, down from once every two weeks in 1987. As we've grown exponentially dependent on our smart phones, I assume these numbers have only decreased since then.

> AS SOMEONE WHO IS CONSTANTLY SOLICITED BY SALESPEOPLE IN MY JOB, TO THIS DAY I HAVE NEVER RECEIVED A HANDWRITTEN NOTE. THAT'S HARD TO BELIEVE AND ALSO A LITTLE DEPRESSING.

Today, marketers have replaced junk snail mail with junk email. It takes seconds to use a mail merge and give the illusion of "customization." It's free and it's SPAM! We all get way too much of it every day, and as a result, we've become completely desensitized to that little blue or red bubble signaling new mail. Most of us don't even see it anymore. Worse, we find getting new email to be a nuisance.

This is why handwritten notes are so effective at grabbing the attention of your potential buyers.

The power of handwritten notes is no secret, and plenty of people will nod their head with a, "Yeah, yeah, I've heard that one before." They're the people who give you one of those pacifying flips of their hand when you bring up the idea.

And then they won't do it.

So why don't more people use them? Because it requires time, money and effort! It's not for the lazy.

Here are some situations that inspire me to craft a handwritten note:

- To grab the attention of a potential customer (rather than cold calling)
- To thank a customer for agreeing to meet with me in person
- To thank a customer/potential customer for talking with me
- In conjunction with a piece of content that is of value to their business (such as accompanying a piece of literature or marketing material)
- To thank a customer for buying my product
- To thank a customer on the anniversary of buying my product
- To wish a customer a happy birthday
- To re-churn the waters and catch the attention of a prospect who told me to check back in a few months
- To follow up after meeting at a networking event or convention

There really is no limit to the good that old-fashioned handwritten notes can do. Try them out and see for yourself. Eventually, everything comes back into style, and I think it's time for handwritten notes to experience their renaissance.

2. Use a Video Introduction

While a handwritten note is no doubt an attention grabber, it's difficult to make a lasting impression through written text.

Humans are hardwired to avoid mental strain, especially when the stimulus is not directly related to their priorities. Consider the heavy lifting your brain must do when reading an article versus watching a video.

It's this inherent laziness that drives us to click on the YouTube video instead of the text-heavy article in the Google results.

Our preference for watching instead of reading is why top venture capital firm Kliner Perkins estimates that video will soon represent 74 percent of all Internet traffic.[9]

While our marketing counterparts have figured out the power of video, salespeople have not.

It's time to start using video to stand out from all the noise.

Think about the email you just sent to your Biggest Fish. Imagine them seeing your message hit their inbox and then imagine them opening it. Now ask yourself this:

If he even opened it at all, how much effort did Mr. Big Fish have to put into understanding who you are, what you do, and most importantly, what you can do for him?

I can answer that for you.

Way too much!

Your email was meant to inspire action in the recipient. Yet it requires the recipient to unscramble your text and become motivated to *change*. The "change" can be a shift from his current competitive solution or the realization that he has an unsolved problem.

That's a whole lot of responsibility being placed onto the shoulders of a crappy email.

You need to be the solution (and maybe you are the perfect solution), but I hate to break it to you—you're not a priority! How do you become a priority? Shock the buyer's system.

---

9   Meeker, Mary. "Internet Trends 2017—Codes Conference." Kleiner Perkins, May 31, 2017. Accessed via www.kpcb.com/internet-trends.

You can only shock the system with something different, some-thing they've never experienced before. It's 100 degrees out, and you jump into a 100-degree pool. Is that refreshing? Does it shock your sys-tem? Hell no! When you send the same email over and over, you lull the recipient to sleep.

If it's 100 degrees out and you jump into a 60-degree pool—now that's shocking!

I use video to shock buyers into noticing me and entice them to give me a shot with a face-to-face meeting or at least a phone call. I know what you're thinking, and you're right, creating a video is much more labor intensive than copying and pasting the same text into an email.

But it's also more fun, more effective and more original because *nobody* else is doing it. Let's walk through the simple but effective process:

1. First, I create a short video (less than one minute). Visit www.knuckledraggingsales.com/book to download a free swipe file with sample script templates I've used to create my videos for prospects.

2. Once I've created the video, I post it to YouTube and email the link to the customer. Visit www.knuckledraggingsales.com/book for a video on how I create, upload and share my videos with potential customers.

3. Half the time, recipients don't view my video via email. I know this because I use software that tracks open and view rates. If they hav-en't viewed it within the first week, I save it to a thumb-drive and snail-mail it to the recipient, accompanied by a handwritten note.

Using the combination of email and snail-mail, I have a 100 percent response rate to my video introductions.

Sometimes the response is, "Not interested at this time." But that just means I can cross them off and move on to the next Big Fish who *is* interested.

Video is not easy, and it's definitely not for the lazy. It's why I began this book by telling you that being a knuckle-dragging salesperson is not for everybody. But if you're hungry and determined to find yourself in a seven-figure sales position, this tactic will work for you.

3. Engage in Social Studying

Businesses and buyers are increasingly using social media to build their brand and communicate with the world. Hidden within their shares and comments are the pearls that salespeople can use to identify selling opportunities, develop connections and even uncover disappointment with their current vendors.

Social Studying requires patience, certain tools, and most importantly, effective listening skills!

That's a tough one, I know.

As salespeople, we're conflicted about when to listen and when to speak. We default to speaking because nobody has ever sold anything by listening 100 percent of the time.

We sit through countless hours of sales training on "what to say." We practice our sales pitch over and over. We try to perfect the timing and deliver it with flawless execution. We memorize our ten-second value-proposition so that when we get that rare hallway encounter, we nail it.

CHECK IT OUT ONLINE We also have ridiculous ideas of what a "sales hero" looks like from movie characters and their inspirational sales pitches. Think of the "reco scene" from *Boiler Room*, the "cold calling scene" from *The Pursuit of Happyness* and the "stick your head up a bull's ass scene" from *Tommy Boy* (visit www.knuckledraggingsales.com/book to watch).

All of these scenes are memorable because Hollywood's portrayal of sales is about what you *say*, not what you *hear*. These scenes teach us that it's all about being slick and having the right word tracks spilling out of our mouths.

Somewhere in the sales evolution, an author came up with the trick of asking questions to tease out selling opportunities. Ask enough questions, and the buyer will tell you their problem or motivation for change.

Here's the problem—this does not work!

If you're a buyer, does being probed sound appealing? Aliens probe humans. Humans don't probe other humans.

What's worse is that when you probe, you're asking the same tired questions your competition asks. ("What keeps you up at night?")

You're also asking questions that anyone who studied the buyer's business should know. ("What does a successful year look like?")

You're asking questions that you should *already* have the answer to if you are following them, their company and their industry online. ("What are your biggest pain points?")

As a part of my day job, salespeople are constantly pitching me. When I hear questions like, "What keeps you up at night?" my inner dialogue says, "Wow, this salesperson is lazy. He hasn't done any research into my company, my industry or me!"

Your buyers or someone from their company has already posted the answer to these questions online. The answers might even be on social media. If your target is a publicly traded company, listen to their earnings call. If it's a private company, a quick Google or Twitter search will yield articles guaranteed to answer these questions.

Prior to emailing or calling a potential buyer, spend time studying their social profiles and look for pearls that you can refer to in your video, email or phone call (an action we'll cover in more detail in Chapter

Eight). Here are the business hot buttons I look for *before* I make a call, create a video or craft an email:

- **Strategic imperatives.** That's just a fancy term for top priorities. If possible, listen for cues specific to the target buyer in addition to the CEO.
- **Pain points.** What are the headwinds the business is facing? Does the business have problems that your product or service can address? What problems are they facing that are unrelated to your product where you can help provide insight?
- **Strategic partners.** What companies have they partnered with? Who do they work closely with? Can their strategic partner be a reference?
- **Acquisitions.** Did they make a recent acquisition or were they acquired recently? Can your product help with the integration?
- **Big customer wins.** Have they had any big, publicized wins recently? If so, you can reach out by congratulating them on the accomplishment. How did they win that customer or account? How did they differentiate from the competition? Can your product or service help them further distinguish themselves?

Consider those moments in your day when you meet with a prospect for the first time. As salespeople, we're conditioned to probe for something in common. Maybe it's a picture in a prospect's office that tells you she likes to vacation at the beach or golf. Perhaps a prospective client has kids the same age as your own. Maybe he lives in the town where you grew up.

This search for a connection occurs naturally when we're face-to-face. It shouldn't stop when using other forms of communication.

Do your prospective clients a huge favor and try these techniques. Write notes. Send videos. When the videos fail, send the video in the mail with a note.

Most importantly, don't be lazy. Don't pick up the phone or walk into a prospect's office without doing a little Social Studying first. It's really not that hard.

Social media is a wonderful gift bestowed upon salespeople that reveals buyer likes, dislikes, interests and priorities, all with a shiny bow on top. Accept the damn gift.

Do these techniques require effort? Yes.

Should you do them for every prospect, qualified or not? No.

Do they require a little investment of both time and money? Yes.

Are they memorable? Absolutely.

You don't have to have a sexy product. You don't have to have a product or service that sells itself. You just need to be someone worthy of being remembered.

You have the large hooks, the clubs and the spears already in your possession. Stop politely asking the Big Fish to jump into your boat and surrender. Use the right tools to get the job done.

"*Product experts* are obsolete
because anyone can Google product specs.
Become an *expert in your buyers' business*,
and you'll have customers for life."

John Crowley

CHAPTER SEVEN

LEARN THE BUSINESS AND THE DOLLARS WILL FOLLOW

Anytime I hear people describing their job as "easy money," the first thought that pops into my head is some combination of the following:

1. They are liars.

2. They aren't good at their job.

3. They don't make much money.

Our jobs *can* get easier over time as we learn and perfect the trade, but I hate to break it to you—making *lots* of money is not easy. If it were, a whole lot more salespeople would be rich.

That brings me to my next point, which is the idea of learning lessons *the hard way* versus *the easy way*. Is there really an easy way to learn lessons? If there is, I've never been lucky enough to experience it.

Hard lessons are the only ones that stick. Let's go back to our caveman friends. How did they learn what worked and what didn't? Lots of hard lessons, most of which resulted in their early demise.

Spears not sharpened enough? I bet they found that out pretty quickly. Fire starting technique not effective? Consider that a lesson learned after the family freezes to death.

I'm painting a bleak picture of the future, I know. As a salesperson, are you destined to head down a long road full of nothing but hard, painful lessons?

Even if you are doing the real work of a knuckle-dragging salesperson, you will still mess up. But there's one way to avoid a constant stream of mistakes, and that is to learn from people who already made them.

In fact, that is the *only possible way* to avoid many crushing, demoralizing mistakes that eventually lead you to quit and find an easier job.

Yes, even with help, you'll still make some mistakes of your own. But you'll make fewer mistakes.

Learn from your mistakes and take the successes for what they are—tick marks along the way that let you know you're on the right path. But keep your guard up at all times.

"DUDE, IT'S NOT FOR EVERYBODY"

One of the hardest lessons I've been fortunate to learn came six months into my job as a Distributor Sales Rep. Drunk off more commission than I had ever made in my life, I was all ears when we were offered up a SPIF (Sales Performance Incentive Fund) on increased sales of one particular drug. I immediately went into strategy mode, planning how to blow out my commission and have my first seven-figure year.

I had already failed and learned enough to realize that the quickest way to accomplish a big goal was to talk to people who had already climbed the mountain. So I called Jeff Lovesy, my close friend and mentor.

Lovesy was the guy I always looked up to. He and I had worked together when I was a college intern at a little generic pharmaceutical company in New Jersey. He was the revered Outside Sales Rep, and I was the lonely, confused intern.

It was Lovesy who brought me to the distribution company and convinced them to give me a shot despite my lack of relevant experience. Lovesy took me under his wing, helped me break bad habits I'd picked up in pharmaceutical sales and looked out for me.

I'll never forget our phone conversation about that SPIF. Lovesy meticulously walked me through his targeting process. He outlined how to position the product to different customer segments. He shared advice on leveraging contracts so customers would buy as much as possible. He was a selling genius.

He ended the conversation by saying, "Crowley, be careful. This product isn't for all customers." I hung up and got to work.

Over the next month, I followed Lovesy's advice and the results showed. I won the lucrative SPIF by a mile and was so proud of my accomplishment. Lovesy was the first to call and congratulate me. The credit really belonged to him. Without his insight, I wouldn't have even moved the needle.

I was happy but also perplexed. Lovesy had given me the secret to SPIF success, yet Lovesy himself had finished in the middle of the pack. He *never* finished in the middle. He won everything!

When I asked what happened, he simply said, "Buddy, the product really isn't for everyone."

Huh? I didn't get it.

Ninety days later, I got it. Several of the practices I had convinced to buy huge volumes of the product were irate because their patients' health insurance wasn't paying for the product. These customers now had hundreds of thousands of dollars in inventory sitting on their shelves, slowly expiring because the insurance companies wouldn't reimburse them.

I called Lovesy for more advice. In his cool, calm, West Coast demeanor, he reiterated a saying he'd preached a hundred times before, but which I never understood until that moment:

"Learn the business, and the dollars will follow."

What Lovesy had unsuccessfully tried to pound into my thick skull was the importance of understanding the customers' businesses. Being a product expert isn't enough.

There was a large and influential insurance company in my territory that had decided not to pay for the medicine. My customers bought the drug. The physicians prescribed the drug. But insurance wouldn't pay for the drug. I had failed to learn the ins and outs of my customers' insurance coverage—and that oversight cost them dearly.

The people I had convinced to buy the product were now in jeopardy of losing their jobs. The doctors were understandably furious with my company and me.

In the end, I lost three solid customers because I didn't understand their business or how it worked. While I made serious bank on that one SPIF, I paid the price in the long run by losing credit for those three customers' entire book of business.

DEATH OF A SALESMAN

It was a tough lesson, but one that I was grateful for because it molded my sales philosophy. After SpifGate, I vowed to learn as much as possible about my customers' businesses. I spent countless hours understanding the back office operations, reading about the clinical benefits of all products (not just mine) and uncovering problems totally unrelated to my products.

By taking the time to learn my customers' businesses, I built credibility. I evolved from just another sales rep to a consultant. I was trusted.

Over time, something magical happened.

I quit cold calling.

Word spread inside and outside my territory about how I could help practices save money, add novel revenue streams and run their business more efficiently.

Prospective customers then started calling me! They had heard what I was doing for other customers and came to me for consultation.

Eventually I would get to a sales pitch, *but* I didn't have to talk about price anymore. I had created so much value outside of my day job that customers were willing to pay a higher price for my products in order to work with me.

It was *miraculous* . . . except there was nothing miraculous about it. I had worked hard to get to that point by learning all about my customers' business. I understood what made them tick, what motivated them and what mattered most to their bottom line rather than my own.

How did I make the transition? I quit selling and started asking questions unrelated to my product. Yes, this is a sales book, and I'm telling you to quit selling.

The quality of your career is not related to your product prowess, how many closing techniques you've memorized, your suit, your smile, your product, your pitch or your price. It's about knowing your customer base well enough to ask questions that matter—not to you, but to them.

As Tony Robbins says, "The quality of your life is directly related to the quality of your questions."

Most likely, you've spent countless hours in sales training. You've been taught everything about your product and the competitors. You've been coached on how to asking probing questions that "agitate unknown problems" and "uncover hidden opportunities" to position your product.

All of this is a necessary part of learning the ropes of our trade. After training, you're on your own. And that's unfortunate because most companies' sales training stops right before they get to the stuff that really matters, which is the business of your customer.

I've been in sales my entire adult life. I obviously appreciate the sales rep's struggle because I've walked in those shoes and now train others to bravely forge that path. Yet, as a buyer, I don't have an iota of patience for salespeople! It's no wonder our sales-naïve customers despise us. It's because 99 percent of sales reps are selling to benefit themselves, not the customer.

Your ability to be an encyclopedia of knowledge about your product is frankly not all that useful anymore. Understand your customer's business, because only then can you offer to *improve* their business.

In my experience, the vast majority of customers across all industries know how to use this thing called the Internet. All they have to do is click a few buttons and an endless stream of information comes vomiting out of their computer screen about whatever gadget, gizmo, software, drug or service they're after.

Don't offer them boring selling points about your product that they can get in two seconds from Google. Offer them far, far more. Consider ways to make their jobs better and their work lives easier! Do that, and you will never be forgotten. You'll also find that over time, your job will become exponentially easier.

LOOKING OUT FOR #1 SUCKS

How do you learn about your customer's business? First, don't let your *training* get in the way of your *education*.

Most training programs look through the lens of their own company, not the customer's. You do need to master your product and process. But once you have, it's time to focus on learning about your customers.

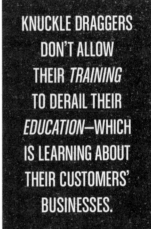

KNUCKLE DRAGGERS DON'T ALLOW THEIR *TRAINING* TO DERAIL THEIR *EDUCATION*—WHICH IS LEARNING ABOUT THEIR CUSTOMERS' BUSINESSES.

You're going to start where you'd start with your own business. Like Rod Tidwell said in *Jerry McGuire*, we all want someone to show us the money. So first you need to identify and follow the flow of money for your customers.

- **How do they make money?**
- **Where do they make the most money?**
- **Where do they lose money?**
- **What are their biggest cost drivers?**
- **What part of their business relies on forces outside of their control?**

The goal isn't to solve every problem. The point is to relate to their struggles and to speak to their business in a way that demonstrates you're there to become a long-term partner in their business rather than a mere transaction conduit.

In case you don't already realize this, your customers don't care about you hitting quota. That's your problem, not theirs. They have their own problems. If you can help them with those, you've got a friend and customer for life.

No customer cares more about you or your product than they care about their own business. Here are some ways you can begin to learn about what matters to *them*:

1. Practice Preceptorships

In the medical field, preceptorships are a routine practice where medical students shadow a practicing physician and quietly observe interactions with patients. This type of activity is the absolute best way to learn you customer's business! Here's how this works for salespeople:

1. Identify every person/role at your customer's business who is involved in the buying process, implementation process and post-purchase maintenance of your product or service.

2. Spend half a day observing each of these people at work. What are their pain points? What processes don't make sense? Where are there redundancies or inefficiencies?

3. The purpose of a preceptorship is to learn, *not sell*. Be empathetic. Ask quality questions. Listen and never, ever sell!

Has any salesperson ever asked to get to know your business (or even what your job title means you actually do all day)? Has anyone who has ever tried to sell you anything asked questions about what matters to you and *then* followed through by getting to know your daily operations, how you make money and your pain points?

Of course not!

What would you think if someone wanted to dig in and get to know your business with no strings attached? You'd be humbled, flattered and eager to hear what insights this person has for your business. Human beings are inherently egocentric; we love it when people take an interest in us and make us feel like more than just a number.

Life and all of its transactions are getting much, much faster. Be the professional who slows down and stops selling long enough to get to know others. This takes time and patience, but it's also simple. *And* it delivers long-term results rather than short-term, fleeting gains.

2. Hang with the Cool Kids

Every industry meeting has an exhibitor hall. As salespeople, we're often relegated to working the booth, which is a laborious and boring task. We're often stuck conversing with customers that aren't in our territory. Rather than hanging at the booth during sessions or fraternizing with colleagues in the hallway, hang out with the cool kids—your customers!

Stop viewing trade shows and other industry meetings as a waste of time. See them as an opportunity to build your reputation as an expert in the business of your customers. Here are some suggestions:

- Sit in on sessions with your customers regardless if they're relevant to your product.

- Demonstrate that you're more than "just a rep" by asking quality questions to the speakers. Before meetings, connect with and engage speakers. Educate yourself on their speaking subject and come prepared with questions. Download my "Conference Checklist" at www.knuckledraggingsales.com/book to see my process for preparing and having a rewarding conference experience.

CHECK IT OUT ONLINE

- Don't get sucked into the trap of hanging with your colleagues at customer meetings. Meetings are exhausting enough already. Why not use the time to maximize customer exposure?

- Make the most of your time by going to dinner, meeting for drinks and socializing with your customers rather than your buddies. If you need to see friends more often, schedule outside-of-work time instead of wasting valuable customer face time to fraternize.

3. Follow Your Customer's Playlist

Tuning in to what people watch, listen to and read is another great way to discover what matters most to them. For example, I don't watch TV, so when someone asks, "Did you see *Dancing with the Stars* last night?" I immediately know this is not one of my people.

However, if someone asks if I read the new Anthony Iannarino book, my ears perk up because I know this is someone from my tribe. This person and I are likely to quickly connect on meaningful common ground instead of asking generic questions about their hometown, pets or favorite vacation spots.

Observing the contents of your customer's office may offer insight, but if you can't get to them in person, study what they share or comment about on social media. These are all breadcrumbs leading to your buyers' hearts.

When you engage in this type of activity, you'll start to hear, see and read what genuinely interests your Big Fish. Use this information to engage customers in meaningful conversations—*especially* if it's not directly related to your product.

If you connect on a topic near to your customer's heart, you'll eventually have an opportunity to talk about your product.

To learn about the customer's business, it's important to understand the entire organization. Start at the bottom of the company and ask about their struggles, what scares them and what keeps them from doing the best job possible. Seek to understand how they're compensated and measured in their job. In other words:

"Learn the business . . . and the dollars will follow."

It's not all about being selfless. It's still about the money. But your customers are in the business of making money, too! Why not be the one to help them make more?

Since the days of the cavemen, mankind has been looking out for themselves in order to survive. But we can only *thrive* by forming tribes and building relationships. Take the time to find out what you can do to make the jobs of others more effective, whether it be stick gathering, cave drawing, fur trapping or hunting. Do that, and everyone in your tribe benefits.

"Social media can't close the sale.
But it can do a whole lot
to get you through the door."

John Crowley

CHAPTER EIGHT

ACCESS SELLING

C an you imagine what our primitive ancestors would think if they were given a glimpse into today and saw all these well-shaven, sweet-smelling people hypnotized by tiny glowing screens in front of their faces?

We live in a world where everyone from toddlers to grandparents is on social media. As a salesperson, you know you're supposed to be sending LinkedIn connection requests to potential customers. You know you're supposed to follow your buyers and their companies on Twitter. You know that blogging will help establish yourself as an expert in your field.

If you're like most people in sales, I also bet you have a decent list of online connections that have proven to be zero percent helpful to your bottom line.

On the surface, social media seems like a wonderful, magical gift that can make our jobs so much easier, and do the work of prospecting for us, and eliminate the need for cold calls and help us make more money. And maybe end world hunger.

If only we could figure out how to use it.

Social media is the biggest sales tease of all time. Here you are, staring at the actual face of your biggest Big Fish on your computer screen. Yet you still have no clue how to reel him in, or even how to get him to accept your connection request.

In this chapter, we'll dissect the virtual temptress who tantalizes you with promises of increased sales but has failed thus far to deliver.

> ACCESS SELLING WILL RESTORE YOUR FAITH IN SOCIAL MEDIA'S ABILITY TO PUT MORE MONEY IN YOUR BANK ACCOUNT.

The concept of Social Selling has failed to such a degree that many companies and salespeople cringe at the very idea of using social media for anything other than product announcements and giveaways.

And yet access to customers is the #1 problem we have—a problem that social media can fix when used properly! So I've coined the term *Access Selling* instead of Social Selling to help avoid the adverse reaction people have to that term.

Make you feel better? Let's get started.

THE FIRST RULE OF FIGHT CLUB

First, let's define Access Selling in order to gain a better understanding of what it can and cannot do:

Access Selling is the use of social media channels, such as LinkedIn and Twitter, to 1) build meaningful relationships with your customers, 2) differentiate yourself, 3) bypass gatekeepers, 4) speed up the sales process, 5) identify decision makers and 6) deliver value, all with the ultimate goal of increasing profitable sales.

It's an incredibly valuable tool, but in order for it to do its job, there are two rules that must never be broken: The first rule of Access Selling is to *never* sell online. The second rule of Access Selling is to *never* sell online.

This goes back to the reason you don't think social media is helping you close more sales. It doesn't "close more sales" because you can't make a sale on LinkedIn. That's not how this works.

Access Selling is a tool—one of many tools in your little fur-lined tool belt. But it isn't the spear. It's the club. It's designed to get someone's attention, not to go for the kill.

It can help you qualify leads, but once you've qualified a lead, the conversation should move offline. At a minimum, switch the conversation to the phone. If your position allows, shoot for a face-to-face meeting. There are too many tones confused, body language cues missed and opportunities squandered because of electronic and phone conversations.

Nothing beats an in-person sales pitch.

I remember my first sales training class. The lead trainer reminded me of Jim Young, Ben Affleck's character in *Boiler Room*. In a session on rapport building, the Jim Young clone compared building sales rapport to picking up women in a bar. He told us, "You don't just walk up to a woman and ask her to marry you." (His actual pearl of wisdom was a little more crass, but you get the idea.)

His point was that you have to find something in common in order to get her attention. Find out what she's passionate about and get her talking.

Selling requires the same tact. You look for pictures, artifacts and memorabilia in the customer's office and get the buyer talking—especially if you share any of the same interests.

But how do you build rapport if you can't make it past the gatekeeper or get the target to take your call or respond to an email? Unless your client is a doomsday prepper or a conspiracy theorist, chances are this individual has shared something online.

Access Selling empowers you with information to create a connection and build a relationship without cold calling or breaking through the gatekeeper.

Access Selling provides you with a way to connect faster and with a higher success rate. You'll make fewer calls than with the old fashioned smiling and dialing, but each call will have an exponentially higher chance of resulting in the payoff, which is the face-to-face meeting.

I need to add a disclaimer here: done the wrong way, Access Selling could also be called *Creepy Crawling*. There's a fine line between gathering useful information and crossing into online stalker territory.

I stay away from the line by containing the vast majority of my Access Selling activities to LinkedIn, Twitter and Google. It works for me because 74 percent of B2B buyers are on LinkedIn.[10] For the most part, the information on LinkedIn is professional and business oriented. On occasion, I look at other social channels because I can't

10 Source: McKinsey & Company

find the buyer on LinkedIn or can't find enough information to make a connection.

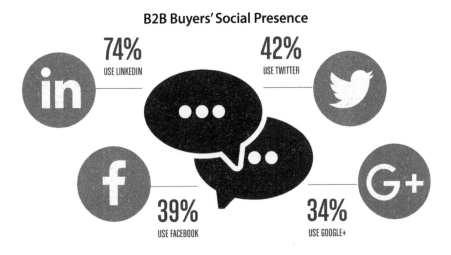

If you check Facebook, Instagram, Snapchat or sites like Pinterest, be aware that these channels are primarily platforms reserved for personal information. I've heard horror stories of sales reps referring to Facebook posts containing scantily clad bikini shots of the buyer's wife. This can cross the creepy line.

SO WHAT *CAN* IT DO?

Access Selling may not close sales online, but it does make the entire sales process more efficient. And like anything, you get better at it with practice. Access Selling empowers you to:

1. Build Relationships

Every day we become more and more detached. Texting and emailing are easier than calling. The more we engage in impersonal forms of communication, the harder it becomes to make meaningful connections. This trend is bad for business because successful operations across all industries thrive on relationships.

Ironically, social media is both to blame for this detachment and also the answer to help overcome it. Taking the time to "virtually listen" to customers and learn their business by reading their profiles, comments and posts helps build rapport before you meet them in person.

2. Stand Out from the Competition

Engaging in Access Selling is also a way to differentiate you from the competition. The reason is simple. Ask any average salesperson if they should be using social media to engage with prospective customers. Their answer will be some form of, "I don't have time for that."

It takes a lot to stand out in a world filled with shiny objects and distractions galore, but you *can* and *will* stand out by learning how to properly engage in Access Selling.

3. Bypass Gatekeepers

Some customers boycott social media. There's not much we can do about that. Access Selling is for those in your target demo who are active online (liking articles and other posts, commenting, etc.). For people who have taken the time to work on their profiles and post content, Access Selling empowers you to strike up a conversation that will get their attention.

Replying with a smiley face on their post won't cut it. If you want to initiate a genuine online discourse that ends with a face-to-face meeting, you have to do what you'd do when you want to grab anyone's attention: Say something interesting and don't be boring.

4. Speed Up the Sales Process

Access Selling enables you to identify opportunities with the prospect or customer (pain points, areas of need, strategic initiatives) earlier in the buying process so that you can speed up your sales process.

This is important because on average, potential buyers reach out to sales reps 70 percent of the way through the buying process.[11]

At this stage, the customer has already realized her problem, researched possible solutions and evaluated the competition. Now she's ready to discuss pricing. Best-case scenario, your product is in the running, and the discussion is purely price. Worst-case, she inaccurately evaluated your product, and you're not even in the race.

5. Identify Decision Makers

Back in the olden days, one of the key steps in the sales process was identifying the decision maker. Due to the complexity of business and changing environment, the decision maker has been replaced with the *buying committee*, where multiple people have varying influence on a buying decision. In the *Challenger Customer*, CEB Global's research uncovered that the average buying committee has 5.4 members. That means you need to identify the 5.4 decision makers and customize your pitch to every one of them. Access Selling helps identify the members of the buying committee and what they value so that you can customize your pitch to each individual.

6. Create Value

Connecting with a potential buyer on social media early on in the process enables you to provide value and foster reciprocity through the sharing of information (directly or indirectly related to your product). Providing unsolicited value is a great way to "warm up" the prospect.

---

11 Corporate Executive Board. www.executiveboard.com/exbd-resources/content/digital-evolution/index.html

When you create value, the prospect learns who you are and can see that you're not the stereotypical selfish salesperson.

When you eventually send an introductory email, make the first call or drop in for a visit, you've already warmed up the prospect. He knows who you are. He may not need your product right now, but when he eventually does, he'll remember you. Because of this existing relationship, he will engage you early in the buying process. That means you'll have the opportunity to more greatly influence his purchasing decision.

This is important because 74 percent of buyers choose the product of the sales rep who is the first to add value![12] *Just as the early bird gets the worm, the early sales professional gets the sale.*

ACCESS SELLING 101

Now you know what Access Selling can do for you—a whole lot. Next I'll explain how to go from staring at a static list of virtual contacts to making meaningful connections. There are three basic steps in the process:

CHECK IT OUT ONLINE

Step 1: Optimize Your LinkedIn Profile

If you have an incomplete LinkedIn profile, buyers are less likely to accept your connection. Without connecting with your clients, you're limited in what you can see on their profiles. Visit www.knuckledraggingsales.com/book to download the infographic, *How to Create a Killer LinkedIn Profile*, on the following pages. Follow these instructions and get your LinkedIn profile shining before you reach out. First impressions are everything.

---

12   Corporate Visions. http://win.corporatevisions.com/rs/corpv/images/CVI-%20CMO%20-Messaging-ebook_v6-interactive.pdf

How to Create a Killer LinkedIn Profile

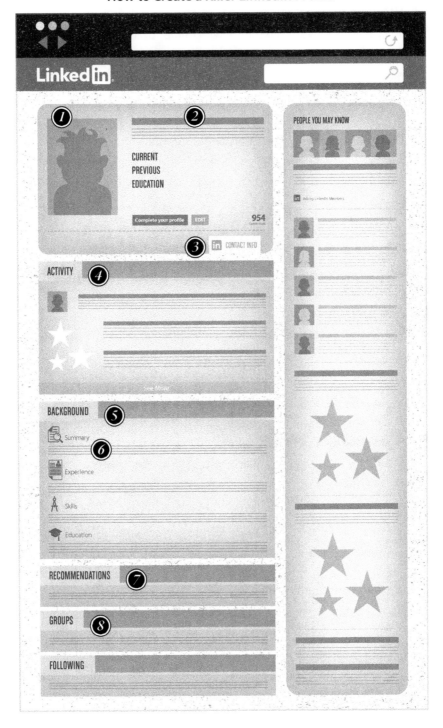

① Use a Professional Photo

You can increase your LinkedIn views 11 times by including a photo. A professional photo is the first step towards humanizing yourself—be more than just an online resume.

② Write a Compelling and Searchable Headline

The headline on your profile will default to your current job title—change it! Next to your name, the headline is the most searchable field on LinkedIn. Use this space to define your personal value proposition—describe the *what* you bring to clients. Utilize key words that a customer looking for a person in your position would search.

③ Add Your Contact Info

People only see your contact information after connecting. You won't get spammed. Don't miss an opportunity to connect with a potential customer because you didn't input your real phone number and email address.

④ Add Media Rich Content (visume, audio, video, or presentations)

The most effective way to inspire a sale is by showing how your product works. Add media that demonstrates the ease or utility of your product. If you sell a service, upload a video of you pitching the product. Media adds dimensions to your personality and product that don't come across in print.

⑤ Write to Your Customers

Do your customers care that you're a "Quota Crusher," "Expert Negotiator" or "President's Club Winner?" *No!* They want to know what value you'll bring to them before they start the buying journey. Create your profile with your customer's needs and wants in mind.

⑥ Be Genuine in Your Summary

The summary section is the perfect place to let your guard down and talk about what motivates and inspires you. The best summaries include a personal mission statement or core set of beliefs.

⑦ Get Recommendations

Ask customers, employers, colleagues, coaches—anyone who can attest to your character at work or within your community—to write a LinkedIn recommendation.

⑧ Join and Engage in Groups

This is the fastest way to gain exposure and recognition on LinkedIn. A quick search of "Healthcare/Medical Sales" will pull up several different groups you should join. By participating in the conversation, you build credibility as a thought leader in your space.

Step 2: Research Connection Points

Pitching a buyer before creating a connection is lazy and rarely works. These days, the true cold call is annoying to a prospect and burns through a perfectly good lead for the sake of meeting your call metric. The same applies to connecting with people on LinkedIn. If you send a generic auto-generated invitation to a prospect, you're missing your chance to make a more meaningful connection.

Here's the process I follow when researching a buyer's LinkedIn profile. This process enables me to find connection points *before* I send the request:

1. Name. Search for the prospect's name on LinkedIn.

2. **Mutual Connections.** Look at your mutual connections. Your geographical location and people you have in common are the two easiest ways to connect on LinkedIn.

3. **Summary.** The summary section of LinkedIn is intended to be an overview of the person, not their career. It's where they talk about what motivates and inspires them. It's where they can add personality to their profile. Unfortunately, most people don't know how to optimize their profile, and this area is often left blank or is a synopsis of their resume. Don't do that.

> QUESTIONS TO ASK ABOUT YOUR BUYERS' LINKEDIN ACTIVITY:
>
> •ARE THE ARTICLES THEY READ ALL ABOUT THEIR INDUSTRY?
>
> •DO THEIR LIKES ALL HAVE A RUNNING THEME?
>
> •WHAT KINDS OF POSTS DO THEY SHARE MOST OFTEN?
>
> •DO THEY LIKE OR FOLLOW THE POSTS OF ANY OF THE SAME PEOPLE YOU LIKE?

4. **Activity.** This section shows articles they've written, content they've posted and articles they've liked or commented on. Pay particular attention to their articles. Anyone who takes the time to write an article and has the courage to post it on a public forum must be passionate. You can also use articles they've liked or commented on as insight into what they're thinking about these days.

5. **Media.** Posting videos and slide presentations on LinkedIn is one way to increase your profile visibility. Look for these types of media within profiles, as they often contain points of view that help you understand what the buyer values.

A complete profile can be rich with connection points. These are my five favorite areas, but don't limit yourself to just these. Search on!

Step 3: Always Be Connecting

Now that you know the buyer's interests, it's time to connect. Relying on the generic LinkedIn connection—"Lazy Person wants to add you to their LinkedIn network"—is an absolute *no*!

Generic requests are SPAM, and many people will not accept them. As a buyer, I've been burned by accepting a generic request. I immediately get hit with a follow-up email asking for 30 minutes to pitch their product. This is not how professionals use LinkedIn.

Personalize your greeting by referring to one of the connection points listed above. Conclude with, "I'd like to connect and learn from you."

When the buyer accepts your invitation, resist the temptation to follow up with an email asking for anything or trying to sell.

You must create value first!

Step 4: Engage with Insight and Add Value

The final two chapters of this book are all about Step 4. In the next chapter, we'll talk more about how to engage with insight, and the last chapter will explore the concept of "value" during the engagement phase and how to create it.

Before we talk details, let's define what these two things mean.

1. **Engage with Insight.** Engaging with insight means you respond to a prospect's posts and other content in a meaningful way. It's one of the fastest ways to get noticed by your Big Fish. When you comment on your Big Fish's LinkedIn articles and share his content, he receives email updates alerting him of the activity.

   "Who is this person sharing and commenting on my stuff?" he starts to think.

   Then comes the most important part of the process—that is, the "insight" part. The secret to being remembered rather than just noticed is to engage with insight. The lazy way to engage is to write comments like "Great article!" or "Thanks for sharing." While this activity will be captured and emailed to your Big Fish, it doesn't incite a response.

To be remembered, make insightful comments that specifically call out parts of the article you found particularly helpful. Ask a question about something you didn't understand or ask for input on a problem you're experiencing relative to the article.

Want to really be remembered? Take a respectful counterstance to your Big Fish's opinion. Disagree with the point of the article and explain why you disagree. More on this in the next chapter.

2. **The "Value" Buzzword.** There's so much talk these days about "creating value." The problem with "value" is that it doesn't mean the same thing to everybody. When it comes to selling to a buying committee, this can be a huge problem. Buyer #1 may value something completely different from buyer #2. So whose value is more important? And how do you know who values what?

All members of the buying committee are involved in the decision-making process, but they're buying the same product for different reasons. For example, when selling a technology into a health system, the CIO will value security, the CFO will value cost savings and the CEO will value the impact it has on company strategy.

Access Selling is the best tool for identifying what's important to each member of the buying committee. It will allow you to tailor your approach and presentation to include what matters to all members who have a say in the decision.

Using the same three-step process you followed in the "Different is Better" chapter (use handwritten notes, video and social media profiling), you can reach out to each buyer by leading with one of the hot button issues you discovered on their social media pages. And this time, you're going to research solutions to these concerns.

I can hear you now. "What if my product doesn't solve these problems?" That's great! Offering solutions that have nothing to do with your product is the fastest way to create value, become a trusted advisor and build credibility for your future sale.

Here are some examples of ways to create value other than through what you sell. Let's pretend you sell birth control pills to OB-GYNs (my first job out of college):

- **Hone in on strategic priorities.** Your research uncovers that your Biggest Fish is in the process of opening a Women's Sexual Treatment Center to help women suffering from sexual dysfunction (true story). You see they have several nursing jobs posted on LinkedIn. You know some nurses who are tired of working for the hospital down the street and are looking for a change of pace. You forward your Big Fish the LinkedIn profiles of the nurses with a note that says:

  > *Dear Dr. Big Fish,*
  > *Congrats on the Women's Sexual Treatment Center open-ing! I saw that you're looking for nurses with obstetrical experience. I'm sending you the profiles of Nurse Betty and Nurse Sue. I've known them for five years, and they're amazing because blah, blah, blah.*
  > *Warmly,*
  > *Knuckle Dragger*

  You've created value for Dr. Big Fish, saved her time recruit-ing and saved her money by not having to pay a recruiter. You've also created goodwill with Nurse Betty and Nurse Sue because you helped them find a new rewarding career.

- **Identify pain points.** Medicare announces a cut in physician payments. The cut is so deep that it threatens the financial viability of all OB-GYNs. One of your existing customers raves about a webinar series on cost-cutting strategies for OB-GYNs. You email Dr. Big Fish with the webinar details and a note that says something like:

> *Dear Dr. Big Fish,*
> *I have nothing to do with this webinar, but I thought your practice would find the information highly valuable and worth your time.*
> *Best,*
> *Knuckle Dragger*

  While women of childbearing age (potential users of your birth control pills) are too young to qualify for Medicare, you demonstrate that you care about helping the practice, not just about selling more birth control.

- **Help them win.** *Nashville Magazine* has just nominated Dr. Big Fish for "OB-GYN of the Year." The voting takes place electronically, and you can vote once per day for 30 days. You share the voting link with your LinkedIn network several times during the voting period (always tagging @DrBigFish), asking people to vote for Dr. Big Fish. Doctors are typically egotistical, and your efforts don't go unnoticed by your prospect.

Once you engage with insight and create value, you're on your way to moving the conversation offline. Use your best judgment when asking for time to discuss how your product can solve a problem. If you're denied or ignored, it means you haven't created enough value. Go back to Step 4 and add more value and engage with more insight. Rinse and repeat.

HOW ACCESS SELLING CAN FAIL

Access Selling is not an excuse to spend all day on LinkedIn. It's not a replacement for calling on prospects. Unfortunately, its allure is too compelling for many to resist, and before they know it, they spend prime selling hours trolling the Internet and getting nothing accomplished.

For this reason, I recommend that you pilot Access Selling on half of your Big Fish. This trial will demonstrate the effectiveness of Access Selling for your business and can serve as a useful case to implement the most effective Access Selling tactics across the entire sales force.

Old school sales managers may frown upon any sales activity that doesn't include traditional email blasts, dialing for dollars and pounding the pavement. If this sounds like your boss, tell him/her about this new Access Selling technique that you're going to test out on your Big Fish.

The timing of your online activities is less important than consistency. My recommendation is to pick one hour a day (I like first thing in the morning) and schedule it on your calendar so that it happens every day. Make Access Selling a habit. The worst time to engage in Access Selling is during prime selling hours.

Keep track of how many virtual connections lead to actual, legitimate connections (either on the phone or face-to-face with the decision maker). Tracking these results and coming up with useful percentages is the only way to determine whether Access Selling is worth your time.

Wondering if all of this really works? LinkedIn recently conducted a study about the correlation between sales reps who use social networks and the impact of quota attainment.

They found that 78 percent of salespeople actively using social networks outperformed their peers.[13]

As useful as social media can be, it's not the silver bullet of sales success because there are no secret pills or magic recipes. The secret to sales success is to just keep fighting! Get up early, run (don't walk) out of your cave, and start attacking the day like you mean it. Use Access Selling to help you operate with more efficiency and to connect with others in a way that matters to them and makes you more money.

13　Source: LinkedIn. https://business.linkedin.com/sales-solutions

"When used properly,
Engaging with Insight can get your
target buyer off the screen and
on the phone—and eventually face-to-face."

John Crowley

CHAPTER NINE

ENGAGING WITH INSIGHT

According to an article in *The Telegraph*, scientists are now claiming that Neanderthals were not as dim-witted as we once believed. In fact, the title of the article is "Neanderthals Were Too Smart for Their Own Good." New research suggests that they died out because they were *too* clever and insightful.

The article explains that by the Ice Age, both our ancestors (the Homo sapiens) and the Neanderthals were roaming around looking for food. Apparently, the knuckle draggers impressed the early humans so much with their skills that humans came to see them as potential mates. Over the course of the next couple of millennia, the ancestors of modern humans slowly "absorbed" the Neanderthals until their recognizable traits were all but gone.

With their short, stocky bodies and protruding brow bones, that love matchup probably sounds unappealing to most of us. But it was their amazing insight into how the world worked (the things they could do with fire are just now being fully uncovered) that won over the hearts of our ancestors.

The Neanderthals had highly advanced tools and weapons. They also had tremendous comprehension of how to survive in the cold through the use of teepee-style huts constructed from mammoth bones and animal skin coverings. All of their insights into survival proved to be highly attractive to our ancestors.

The takeaway?

A little insight can go a long way.

Too bad they didn't have the foresight to see that widespread cross-breeding would eventually wipe them out as a distinguishable species.

Obviously, for the purposes of this book, we're not looking to impress potential suitors. We *do*, however, want to learn how to use our insights to gain the attention of prospects.

Is this even possible in a day and age when there's an endless stream of information coming at us at all times?

Yes!

Let's talk about what insight is and how you can use it to attract more Homo sapiens to what you have to offer.

WALK THE TALK

The formal definition of *insight* is "the capacity to gain an accurate and deep intuitive understanding of a person or thing."

That's profound stuff. How can you convince would-be customers that you're in possession of such a deeply meaningful attribute?

You'd be surprised how little it takes. At first glance, it's counterintuitive to think you can connect with a person electronically and gain a true understanding of that person and what causes them to take action.

But the fact is that very few of your competitors are business experts or customer experts. At best, they're product experts. If you can develop even the slightest insight into how your customers operate their businesses, you're light years ahead of the competition.

> **Engaging with Insight** is a critical step in the Access Selling roadmap. It allows sales professionals to identify topics of interest to buyers and engage in a discussion (online or offline) that demonstrates a sales rep's expertise and ability to provide value. It's about standing out and being different in a way other than sheer persistence.

Engaging with Insight turns the focus toward the customer and away from you and your product. In order to better describe how it works, let me explain how *not* to engage with insight (brought to you by yours truly) and how I turned it around.

I had been courting a potential business partner for almost a year. The target company was in an adjacent and desirable space to mine. From the buyer's first-glance perspective, my company had very little to offer her, which meant she held the leverage.

We communicated via email a few times, but nothing of substance. I still hadn't been able to convince her to take a call from me.

I decided to take things up a notch. I flew across the country to "pop in" and catch her at her office. If I was motivated enough to fly across the country on the chance that I could meet with her for 15 minutes, she'd see I was serious. At least that's what I thought.

I stood in her lobby, anxiously awaiting the receptionist's response to my bold, daring, attention-grabbing maneuver. I grew nervous that I'd just wasted a thousand dollars in travel and two days that I could have spent generating revenue.

I was nervous for good reason—somewhere inside, I knew this was a mistake. Sure enough, the receptionist informed me that she was in back-to-back meetings all day and wouldn't be able to meet me.

Damn, back to the drawing board.

On the flight home, I reviewed her LinkedIn profile and saw that she was an active participant in one particular LinkedIn group. She had recently posted several articles about her business's tax troubles. The light bulb went off and I slumped back in my first-class Southwest center seat, disappointed in myself . . .

I had broken my own rule and failed to engage her with insight!

I'd assumed that because I led a multi-million dollar division in a Fortune 15 company, she would be impressed enough to meet with me. Maybe she didn't realize how important I was (that's sarcasm). What an idiot.

I read through the articles she posted on LinkedIn and began commenting. I referred her to other articles outlining deduction options her business could take to offset the tax burden. I connected her with an accountant I had used in the past who helped my company find new tax vehicles. I took a counterstance to a pessimistic update she'd posted complaining about the hopelessness of her business.

That is engaging with insight.

The next day she emailed me, apologizing for not being able to meet but thanking me for the article and accountant connection.

Here was the best part—the partnership I wanted to create with her could be turned into a giant tax deduction for each of us. It would enable her to make a significant investment in her company's growth by driving revenue, and it would provide me with a write-off. It was a win-win-win.

The moral of the story? I could have saved a thousand dollars and lots of valuable time if I would have followed my own advice about engaging with insight and creating value *before* flying across the country.

HOW AND WHY IT'S DIFFERENT

Engaging with Insight isn't necessarily easier than flying across the country to impress someone. In fact, looking back, *that* was actually the lazy route. Engaging with Insight takes active participation. It takes persistence and a fighter's spirit.

If you find Engaging with Insight easy, you're doing it wrong. Lazy sales reps (not sales professionals) respond to their buyers' posts with comments like "thanks for posting" or "great article." This translates into, "I'm stalking you, not reading your posts" or worse, "I'm lazy and not willing to take the time to understand your business."

You know the guy at the company party who's "talking to you" but is constantly scanning the crowd for someone more important? He adds absolutely nothing to the conversation with quips like, "That's too funny," "No way," and "Oh, my god."

You know he's not listening and probably doesn't even remember your name. That's what you're doing when you like someone's content or make a generic filler comment. Engaging with Insight doesn't work like that.

If Engaging with Insight was a guy at a party, he'd be the one everyone wants to talk to. We all want to feel like human beings, not tick marks, and we seek out people who care about us.

Engaging with Insight humanizes online communication. It mimics the time-tested tactics we use when we're face-to-face to establish trust, build rapport, create credibility and ultimately deliver value.

The caveat is it requires more effort than face-to-face rapport building because we have to overcome the limitations of written communication. When communicating through text, we lose the help of physical cues that make it much easier to establish a connection.

Unlike typical online interactions, Engaging with Insight fosters reciprocity. That's because the insight you provide speaks to a prospect's "What's in it for me?" (or WIIFM). People care about themselves first and foremost. Until you can provide them with something of value, why would they give you a moment of their time?

You haven't earned it, and frankly, you don't deserve it.

The goal of all this is the same as the goal of Access Selling—to move the conversation from an electronic forum to the phone or face-to-face, where sales are made and long-term mutually beneficial relationships are formed.

SO HOW DO YOU DO IT?

Engaging with Insight starts with listening. It requires empathy. It also mandates that you are *serving* your buyer, not *selling* your buyer. If you have a servant's mindset, you understand the value of helping your customers, regardless of you personally benefitting.

> ENGAGING WITH INSIGHT MEANS YOU SERVE YOUR BUYER, NOT SELL YOUR BUYER.

The idea of Engaging with Insight is not a new one. It's been happening in sales for a long time. It just looks different now, thanks to the fact that so much of what we do and how we communicate is online.

The most primitive version is finding a piece of memorabilia in your buyer's office and getting him talking about it.

Where did you catch that huge fish hanging on your wall?

Couldn't help but notice that Yankee hat. Are you a big fan?

Are those your kids? They're beautiful.

Those conversations still need to happen, and the best way to get you there is social media.

Social media provides a window into the world of your buyers. It's a way to see what's important to them. With that insight, you create value by speaking to those priorities and suggesting solutions to their problems.

Without that insight, you're shooting in the dark. You can guess that one prospect is like another, but there's no guarantee.

There are also many ways to engage that don't involve online social networks. If your prospect has been published or cited in the media, you can gain insight into their motives by reading those publications.

Another way to engage a prospect is to start hanging out where they always hang out. It's just like high school. If you want to socialize with the cool kids—go to parties. Jocks—go to the gym. Nerds—join the chess club. What meetings do your potential buyers attend? Are they members of relevant societies or organizations? Join those same organizations.

If you have access to their office, look for periodicals they read. What magazines are in the office or on their desk? Read those journals, and the next time you see them, reference an article you found interesting. If you can't see them, send buyers a link to an article that's of relevance to them or their business.

Spend time learning what your buyer is coping with and seek solutions outside the realm of your product and expertise. With time and effort, even the toughest buyers will appreciate your efforts and see the value you have brought them and their business.

Okay, but how much time? The time commitment depends on the person. In my earlier example, it took just one day (that is, once I realized my mistake).

Some people are guarded and cautious. They don't trust anyone. Others trust everyone until they get let down or disappointed. It all depends on how much value you can provide and if you can strike a chord with the buyer.

HOW I ENGAGE TO ADD TO MY SALES FUNNEL

I created an online course to help young professionals with no experience break into healthcare sales. It's called *No Experience Necessary University*. Instead of spending thousands of dollars on advertising to drive potential customers to my website, I use the Access Selling system.

CHECK IT OUT ONLINE I set up LinkedIn Sales Navigator alerts that notify me of any profiles with text that says things like, "seeking healthcare sales job," "seeking entry level pharmaceutical job," "wanting to break into medical device sales," and so on. Visit www.knuckledraggingsales.com/book for a video of how to set up these alerts.

I've optimized my LinkedIn profile so that anyone who sees it knows I'm the "Healthcare Sales Mentor." This intentional copy explains:

Who I help: healthcare sales professionals and those trying to break into healthcare sales.

What I help them accomplish: break into healthcare sales and sell more products.

Why: so they can enjoy a rewarding and lucrative career.

When I'm alerted to a new keyword-containing profile, I send the following connection request:

"Dear ____, I see you're trying to break into healthcare sales. What is your motivation?"

Ninety percent of the time, they accept my connection and respond with their motives.

Know what else is highly likely? An incomplete profile. Most young professionals are uneducated about the power of LinkedIn and have neglected to optimize their LinkedIn profile.

After connecting, I follow up with this message:

"Dear _____,

Did you know that 91 percent of employers check LinkedIn before reviewing your resume? This means your LinkedIn profile is your first impression. It's also the first place I start when mentoring young professionals like you. Attached is an infographic that I designed to help you optimize your LinkedIn profile to break into healthcare sales."

This simple, one-page document references my website. Most people who receive the infographic will go to my website and sign up for my newsletter. You can download the infographic at www.knuckledraggingsales.com/book.

CHECK IT OUT ONLINE

Once they sign up, they're in my sales funnel and receive a series of emails designed to build trust and eventually convert them to customers of my online program. For those who are unfamiliar, a *sales funnel* is a fancy name someone made up for the buying process. It starts with awareness of you, your company and your product/service and eventually reaches the action phase (aka making a purchase). The idea is that the farther prospects travel down the funnel, the fewer there are. Hence, you filter out the unqualified and keep only those who are bonafide, qualified potential customers.

By using LinkedIn alerts, I'm seeking out the ideal prospects to enter into my sales funnel. Here are the messages I aim to convey in each step of the engagement:

"I am a real person who knows your name." My connection request demonstrates that I've researched them by knowing they want to break into healthcare sales.

"I am credible and have information you need." After we connect, they see my profile, which establishes credibility, defines my target buyer and explains how I can help them.

"I want to know more about what drives you." I get them talking about themselves by asking about their motives. This also provides more insight and helps me understand why they want to break into healthcare sales. Maybe they want to make a lot of money (this is me!). Perhaps they want the freedom that comes from being an outside sales rep. Some want the security of working in an established and growing industry. Others seek the reward that comes from helping patients change their lives. Regardless, that one simple question about motivation helps me understand their why—the single most motivating factor for people. Depending on their response, they're segmented and targeted with email copy speaking to that specific motive.

"I want to help you regardless of whether we ever do business together." By sending them the LinkedIn infographic, I'm creating value and building reciprocity. I ask for nothing in return. I just want them to get value and trust that when the time is right, I can help them.

"I will continue to offer you information that can help solve a problem you have." Once they sign up for my newsletter, they enter my sales funnel, where I talk about how a career in healthcare sales is lucrative, rewarding, flexible and secure. In other words, I'm Engaging with Insight based on the feedback I gleaned from the first communication with them.

This is Engaging with Insight. Everyone feels like they're getting something, and no one gets the feeling they are "being sold."

A "JACK OF ALL TRADES" AIN'T ALWAYS BAD

Have you heard the saying, "Jack of all trades, master of none?" This proverb implies that we have to pick one thing that we're great at or else we'll be mediocre at everything.

When it comes to Engaging with Insight, I have to disagree with this. This mentality does a disservice to salespeople. Now, I'm sure that the caveman who was *the* go-to hunter was awesome. Then there was his neighbor, the guy who was the best at making warm clothes. And of course there was the Neanderthal version of MacGyver—the guy who could make fire by rubbing two sticks together. Everyone loved that guy.

But you know who was even more popular than those guys? The caveman who knew how to do *all* of those things.

Being an expert just in your own field? Sorry, not impressed. Being an expert in your field *and* being able to provide valuable insight to your customers in their fields? Now that is impressive.

It isn't as difficult as it sounds. How did you learn about your field? You studied and read. You talked to people who were already knowledgeable.

Why can't you do the same for your customers? Study and read what your customers are studying and reading. Instead of binge watching the latest season of *The Walking Dead*, spend that time learning and studying your prospects and what they value.

Yes—any learning comes with opportunity cost. That's why the "Jack of all trades" saying came about in the first place. But if you're already an expert in your field and your products, do you really want to spend your time growing a little bit more knowledgeable in your one field over the next year? Wouldn't you rather use that time to learn how to connect with customers across industries?

I'm no tax expert. But I finally reached a Big Fish by researching it for literally just a few hours. I found an article on the Internet written by an expert and used his knowledge to my advantage.

The "fire guy" and the "hunting guru" are great. So are product experts. But the Knuckle Dragger who can provide insights across the board, no matter his or her particular areas of strength? Now that one will survive and thrive!

"Not only does creating value
help increase sales and
decrease the need to cold call,
but it makes the job fun!"

John Crowley

CHAPTER TEN

CREATING VALUE

V*alue* is a word that's tough to define. We could generalize value to mean "something that is useful," "held in high regard" or "has monetary worth." But none of those are all that helpful, at least not when it comes to defining value for a customer.

We're all different. We all share similarities, but it's impossible to apply broad brush strokes to any prospect about what they "value" based on their job title, industry, gender, age or anything else.

Two people working in the same industry, at the same type of company and in the same position may value completely different things. However, there are universal entities that all buyers value, such as their business and their job.

The financial viability of the business is always going to be the top concern. Buyers can have altruistic goals like curing cancer and taking care of patients. But if the business is failing, those other goals can't be accomplished.

It's human nature to protect personal information, especially from salespeople—even if it inhibits those salespeople from providing the best solutions!

I'll give you an example from my own life. I have shot-putter legs. No matter how loose the cut, my legs make every pair of jeans look like yoga pants. I dread shopping for jeans because it always ends with me in a dressing room yelling out, "Still too tight!" after the fitting room attendant has brought me every pair of wide-leg jeans in the store.

I recently came across an article entitled, "How to Buy Jeans for Men with Muscular Legs." The author talked about a new cut of Levi's specifically for guys with tree-trunk quads—the 541 Athletic Cut (this is code for "husky" as an adult). Sweet!

I walked into a department store and was immediately greeted by Taylor Swift's younger, more enthusiastic sister. "Can I help you find something?"

"I'm good, thanks."

I hate shopping. I hate malls. I hate department stores. So why wouldn't I enlist the help of this sweet young lady? I didn't want to be sold. I didn't want her to show me to the Levi's section and proceed to bring me shirts, socks, blazers and belts that matched my brand new 541s.

I would rather prolong my time in the store than be fast-tracked to my destination and be "sold."

We are peppered every day with sales tactics. Online retailers have more information about us than we want to admit. They use that information to tailor their marketing messages. We've grown desensitized to marketing and salespeople in general, and this makes their job even tougher.

Your buyers are no different. If they reveal what they value, they know a decent sales rep will tailor the message to those value points, and they aren't in the mood to be "sold" today.

For that reason, many buyers will protect that information, just like I protected my desire to check out the 541s.

Now, if a salesperson knew I battled thick-thigh-itis and sent me that article preemptively, she would have earned my business for life. I would have bought anything she recommended—because she knew me. She knew what I valued (jeans that don't look like ballerina tights).

How do you identify what someone values outside of a sales meeting? Do your homework. Research them on social media. You'll be shocked what people admit online . . .

 John Crowley @justjohncrowley · 2s ∨
Question, can anyone recommend a cut of #jeans for guys with big thighs? #thickthighssavelives

♡   ⟲   ♡   ⬆

Why would someone share something online for the entire world to see, but not to a salesperson who may be able to help? Because the salesperson is going to recommend the products that will earn him the most commission.

Do you think Taylor Swift's sister can appreciate the plight of thick-thigh-itis? *No!* She only knows what someone from Levi's or corporate told her.

Social media has shrunk our universe. I've never met another guy in person who contends with thick-thigh-itis. But in less than a minute, I can ask a simple question online and reach millions of people across the world who have firsthand experience dealing with thunder thighs. I'm more likely to be vulnerable and share what I value because I know I'll find someone who's coping with the same issue somewhere on the Internet.

Creating value doesn't have to be complicated. In our final chapter, I'm going to show you how—as part of the Access Selling process—even the most primitive brains can learn the difference between product features and benefits and what the prospect truly values.

Spoiler alert: They don't care about your product features or benefits.

WHAT VALUE ISN'T

No doubt you've heard the concept of "creating value" discussed in a sales meeting. So what is it? When I ask sales reps how they provide value, most talk about their product. They confuse *value* with their *value proposition*.

The probability that your product aligns perfectly with your buyer's strategic imperatives is very slim. Your buyers care about three things:

1. **Their career.** Jobs provide buyers with the money to take care of Maslow's needs.

2. **Their reputation.** Bad reputations in business are tough to shake. If a buyer suspects you, your product or your company will sully their reputation, they won't buy from you.

3. **Their company.** The quickest way to get recognized or move up the corporate ladder is to do good things for your company. Show a buyer how to improve their company, and you'll have a customer for life.

Most sales reps (not sales professionals) talk about how their product solves a problem. By eliminating that problem, you provide value, right? *No!*

We create value by solving a problem when it hurts. If I have an itch on my back that I can't reach, and no one is around to scratch it for me, my problem goes unsolved. If I go home that night and my wife offers to scratch the area that used to itch hours ago—that's not solving my problem, either.

Adding value is solving a priority problem precisely when it hurts or itches.

Corporate training has amassed armies of robo-reps. We've replaced problem-solving skills with regurgitated product features and benefits. We train salespeople to fit their square product peg into a round problem hole instead of using common sense.

When all you have is a hammer, everything looks like a nail. Until companies embrace the culture of problem solving and employee empowerment, I fear that adding value will be difficult.

The upshot? For knuckle draggers, this means there isn't much competition at the top of the mountain. While your competitors are busy talking value propositions, you'll be able to provide tangible, time-sensitive value.

WHY VALUE HAS BECOME AN ANNOYING CLICHÉ

I recently joined a rep on a sales call with one of our biggest and most influential customers. The buyer was expressing his frustration with finding qualified pharmacy technicians in his region. This pain had zero overlap with our products but represented a significant opportunity to create value.

The rep immediately went into force-fitting mode and explained how our product would easily fix that problem (it wouldn't). He proceeded to talk about the savings the customer would recognize by using our product and how they could use that money to hire a recruiter.

Oh boy. Swing and a miss.

Later, as we recounted the call, the rep ignorantly proclaimed victory.

Me: How else could you have created value?

Rep: I did create value.

Me: You created a possible solution but you didn't solve the customer's immediate problem.

Rep: What do you mean?

Me: The customer isn't looking for a way to fund a recruiter. He's looking for qualified candidates. What if recruiters burned him in the past and your recommendation irritated him?

Rep: How should I have spun it?

Me: If you have to "spin" your message, you're not creating value. You know several Pharmacy Techs at local hospital XYZ, right?

Rep: Yeah, some really good ones, too.

Me: Are they all happy with their current job?

Rep: No.

Me: Are they your advocates? Are they loyalists to you?

Rep: A couple of them love me!

Me: Get their resumes to your customer!

I went on to tell the rep that this gesture accomplishes four things:

1. You demonstrate to your customer that you listen.

2. You provide a concrete solution to the buyer's problem with no immediate gain for yourself.

3. You create goodwill with your pharmacy technician contacts. Even the technicians who ultimately don't get the job will be indebted to you because you tried to help.

4. You create value for your customer and your pharmacy technician contacts. Both have problems you're attempting to help them solve outside of your day job.

Too many salespeople shoehorn their product as a solution, and the buyer knows they're being "sold to."

It's not working. Rather than *creating* value, shoehorning *erodes* value.

Once a sales professional knows what the customer values, he identifies the best solution—for the customer, not for himself. That's a big and important distinction.

The ordinary sales rep never creates value. He regurgitates features and benefits of his product. A top sales professional figures out what the customer values and helps her find solutions, whether it's his product or something totally unrelated.

The ordinary sales rep hears a problem unrelated to his product or service and thinks, "There's nothing I can do because this has nothing to do with my company." His value creation (if you can even call it that) begins and ends with his product. This is insufficient because finding the right customer at the right time requires *way* too much luck.

A true sales professional creates value in ways that don't involve his product. And when the buyer eventually needs a product, she remembers how the sales professional created value in the past and reaches out to him—not to the sales rep who tried the hard sell last year.

This is *awesome* because it means your timing doesn't have to be spot on! You create so much value that you are never forgotten. When a true need arises for your offering, you'll be the first person to pop into the buyer's head. This is how I was able to stop cold calling after a solid year of providing value to my prospects at every opportunity.

WHY DOES IT MATTER AND WHY SHOULD I CARE?

Your customers are asking that exact same question. They're asking why they should care about *you* or *your* product. They're wondering if you care about them and their business or just yourself and your commission check.

Value creation is providing solutions to your buyer at the *optimal time* (when), in a *highly usable format* (where) and in a *time-sensitive and easily received manner* (how). Here's an example of value creation that includes those three elements:

My company sells pharmaceutical drugs to oncologists. These doctors administer our life-saving drugs to patients with cancer. The doctors then bill the patients' insurance for the drugs and the time it took to inject or infuse them. Most cancer patients are insured through Medicare (government-subsidized insurance for people over the age of 65).

Here's where this gets really interesting. Every quarter, Medicare publishes the reimbursement rates for all FDA-approved drugs online. This information is the lifeline for oncologists because it helps determine which drugs they'll make money on and which drugs will cause them to lose money. Yes, there are life-saving drugs that doctors lose money on by prescribing. It makes no sense, but that's healthcare.

There are three roads a rep can go down at this point:

1. **A typical sales rep** believes he can't impact the reimbursement of drugs. It's his customer's problem, not his. He doesn't bother with knowing the reimbursement or cost of his products.

2. **A self-serving sales** rep goes online to see if the reimbursement for her product changed from the previous quarter. She may or may not alert a customer in the event of a change for fear that a negative slide will impact the use of her product.

3. **A genuine sales professional** (one of the guys on my team took this approach) closely monitors the Medicare website for updates. Immediately upon publication of the rates, he cross-references products with a reimbursement change versus the previous quarter. He then sends his customers and prospects a color-coded Excel spreadsheet sorted by the drugs with the greatest reimbursement changes.

Buyers *love* this service and now anxiously await his quarterly report. It saves them hours of tedious work and helps prevent catastrophic losses.

The report is a solution to a problem that every single oncologist battles. Oncology drugs are incredibly expensive. At the time of writing this book, a new chimeric antigen receptor (CAR) T-cell therapy was just launched with a price tag of $475,000! If this one drug's reimbursement tanked and went unnoticed, it could literally bankrupt a doctor.

The sales rep delivers his report immediately upon the reimbursement rates being published. By sending this at the *optimal time*, it affords his customers enough flexibility to identify affected patients and change them to alternative therapies.

Our competitor provides a similar report in PDF format. By listening to buyers, our rep realized that a PDF prevents the customers from manipulating the data. An Excel spreadsheet delivers the information to them in a *highly usable format*, which enables customers to sort the data and add fields to get more impactful insight.

He then emails the spreadsheet reports since email is the most *time-sensitive and easily received manner* in which to distribute the report to customers.

Sometimes reimbursement decreases are so significant that they can cost an oncologist millions of dollars if not addressed. In those circumstances, our rep emails the report and follows up with a phone call to alert the customer of the significant change. By calling about the problem drug, he creates even more value by preventing the important message from slipping through the cracks (as emails often can).

THE THREE-STEP VALUE CREATION PROCESS

Creating value begins during the prospecting phase of the sales process and never ends as long as you want to keep your customers happy and coming back. Even if you're a "hunter" and only compensated for new business, the value creation responsibilities should transition to those responsible for maintaining the business, such as the account manager or customer service.

Identifying and creating value requires three highly counterintuitive skills for the typical sales rep:

CHECK IT OUT ONLINE

1. Research

The value creation process begins with research. For my business, I use the following Social Studying Process. Download and print this out at www.knuckledraggingsales.com/book. (Then hang it over your computer at your desk.)

The Social Studying Process

GOOGLE

- **Personal website/blog:** What are they passionate about? What inspires them?

- **Company website:** What business are they in? What products/services does their company provide?

- **Press releases:** Recent acquisitions, partnerships, customer wins, etc.?

- **Earning reports:** How is their company performing financially? What are the strategic initiatives of the organization?

LINKEDIN

- **Location:** Do we or did we ever live in similar areas?

- **Summary:** What motivates and inspires them?

- **Articles and posts:** What are their interests?

- **Mutual connections:** Who do they know?

- **Work experience:** Did we work at the same company or in a similar industry?

TWITTER

- **Number of tweets:** When was their last tweet? Is all of the content relevant?

- **Profile URL:** What website do they include in their Twitter profile?

- **Followers in common:** Who do we both know?

- **Retweets and likes:** Who are their influencers?

This is a suggested process based on my business and experience. Depending on where your buyer shares business information, you should use those social media channels in your research.

Many buyers have Facebook, Instagram and Snapchat accounts and will post business- or work-related material that you may find useful in the research process. However, they will also pepper in personal posts. I avoid these more personal channels because I don't want to be caught in a situation where I mention a work-related Instagram post and the buyer realizes she also posted an embarrassing photo.

It gets super uncomfortable for everybody.

It's socially suitable to discuss pretty much anything you find on LinkedIn. Research on LinkedIn is accepted and often welcomed. Research on Facebook, Instagram and Snapchat can be perceived as creepy.

2. Ask Quality Questions

It's vital to quickly convey your intent—to help them, not to advance your sale. Do that by asking quality questions. We talked earlier about what people generally value: their job, reputation and company. Using research you collected in step one, ask questions pertaining to their job, their company and how they want to be perceived in the organization.

Here are some great questions I've heard sales reps ask:

- What are your strategic objectives for this year?

- What is the biggest unsolved problem you're facing?

- What is the biggest unsolved problem your company is facing?

- What is the biggest unsolved problem your boss is facing?

- Do you have any variable components of your job requirements? Are you rewarded or recognized for anything unique in your job? (Both of these questions are meant to discover whether the buyer has any variable components tied to his compensation.)

- Does your boss get rewarded or recognized for similar variable components?

- What are your roles and responsibilities in your organization?

- How can I help you look like a star at your job?

3. Shhhh and Listen Intently

This next step is a huge dilemma for us salespeople. We've been hired for our ability to talk, right? We've been trained to deliver the features and benefits of our products, right?

Wrong!

We're here to serve our customers. You can't serve if you don't know what the customer needs or wants.

Don't confuse listening with waiting for your turn to speak. Listening is genuine. It requires empathy and patience.

IT'S WORTH THE TIME

Looking for opportunities to create value is not for every salesperson. I've rarely had anyone create value for me, but I would certainly be a customer for life if someone ever did.

The fact is no one is doing it. They may say they value their customers, but if they're not creating value outside of what their product "does" for a customer, then they're just saying that to sound progressive and compassionate.

Creating value is one of the only truly win-win scenarios I've encountered in business. Not only does creating value help increase sales and decrease the need to cold call, but it makes the job fun!

Creating value enables you to have genuine discussions rather than uncomfortable one-sided sales pitches day after day, week after week and month after month.

If you're in an inside sales role and are forced to make a certain amount of calls in a day, you won't be able to research every customer. Besides, research can take up all your time if you allow it. I limit the process I just described to 20 minutes per customer.

If you worry you won't have enough time, start by informing your manager that you'd like to try a new technique with your Big Fish. Track the results of your experiment and report those results to your manager.

When you demonstrate the effectiveness of creating value instead of making more cold calls, your manager will be inspired to change.

Whether you're new to sales or have been in the business for a long time, this stuff works. My last pharmaceutical sales job was selling anti-depressants and anti-psychotic medications to psychiatrists while calling on mental institutions. (I have so many terrifying stories!)

All the drugs in these categories were "me-too" drugs. They offered comparable drug efficacy and side-effect profiles, and doctors had no financial ties to the product. Therefore, they typically used the drug of the rep they liked most. It was the ultimate relationship sell.

I was the new guy and hadn't been around long enough to develop the relationships my competitor had garnered during his ten years in the territory. I was screwed.

One day I was waiting in the lobby, hoping to catch the physician long enough to grab his signature and qualify the visit as a call. Dr. Smith was the largest user of my product category in the country. A five percent swing in his market share to my product was enough to skyrocket me into the top rep spot in the country.

As I sat and waited, I overheard the receptionists talking about how Dr. Smith was furious that morning. Apparently, some raccoons had been making a nightly stop by the office to tear apart their trashcans and spew garbage, much as my kids did with their toys in the playroom.

I immediately walked out of the office and drove home without Dr. Smith's signature. I had just received something even more important— I now knew something my prospect valued.

I spent the weekend building a raccoon-proof garbage can shed. On Monday morning, I showed up at Dr. Smith's office bright and early. He arrived to see a sweat-drenched ginger cleaning up the raccoon mess.

As he approached me, I was disappointed to see a look of disgust on his face. Over the six months I had spent in this territory, Dr. Smith had never once graced me with his presence. He was always too busy for me (I hadn't created any value for him). So when I saw him with this expression, I was deflated.

I had just built a shed for him and was cleaning up the trash, and he was thanking me with a church fart face?

I quickly realized that his displeasure wasn't directed at me. It was the raccoons. I introduced myself and showed him his new raccoon-proof fortress. He was blown away!

Dr. Smith: You built this yourself?

Me: Yes sir.

Dr. Smith: Why?

Me: I've been calling on you for six months and never made it past your waiting room. I enjoy helping people and building things. This project accomplished both. I hope you like it.

Dr. Smith brought me into the office through the private back door entrance and granted me lifetime access.

He didn't start using my product that day. However, over the next six months, I fast-tracked the sales process. I exploited my private entrance access to strategically educate Dr. Smith on the benefits of my product in three-minute sound bites.

I didn't get that five percent market share I wanted. Instead, Dr. Smith moved over more than 46 percent, making him the largest user of my product in the country (and the reason I won the President's Award that year).

USE THE RIGHT LURE (NOT MORE BAIT)

Fishing lures are man-made replicas of fish food designed to attract the fish's attention. If you don't fish, you may not know that it's the movement of the lure that grabs the fish's attention more so than its likeness to bait. It's also unlikely that a fisherman can throw a lure precisely in a target fish's line of sight. That's why so many lures are designed to flash, rattle or light up.

> THE "RIGHT LURE" IS MORE ABOUT SUBSTANCE AND LESS ABOUT TIMING.

Typical sales reps use features and benefits like a poorly designed lure. They make lazy attempts to grab the buyer's attention by sending selfish mass emails. When this poorly designed and ill-conceived bait doesn't lure anyone in, sales reps add more lines with more cheap lures to the water, thinking that surely more frenzied activity correlates to more sales.

Along the way, they incessantly talk about their product, neglecting to wait for the "right time" because they fear they might miss their chance.

You have to use the *right* lure, not more lures. The probability of reaching out to a buyer at the precise moment they feel pain that your solution can solve is slim to none. Your buyers have priorities, and those priorities may not align with what you've got to offer—at least not yet.

The whole point is to create value when, where and how the buyer prefers.

Do you want to know why we just spent an entire chapter discussing value creation rather than giving it a brief mention in the Access Selling chapter?

Because 74 percent of B2B buyers choose the product of the sales professional who adds value first.[14]

Let that sink in, because that's an extremely powerful statistic.

I wish I could say to you that if you create value you'll see X percent return on your time. I can't do that. Like weight-loss plans, results may vary. There are too many variables to predict what precise outcome your efforts will receive.

I will say that deliberate and consistent value creation is what eventually helped me stop cold calling. Customers sang my praises to their peers. The positive recommendations generated so much inbound business that I was able to quit prospecting.

Can you be unselfish and highly profitable at the same time? Yes, absolutely you can!

I started this book talking about how money and fear drive the most ambitious salespeople. The ironic part is that only by putting your own

---

14   Source: http://win.corporatevisions.com/rs/corpv/images/CVI- CMO -Messaging-ebook_v6-interactive.pdf

needs aside and lifting up others can you truly achieve the monetary success you desire.

You can also be successful and be selfish—plenty of people are. But there are even more sales to be made by *serving* rather than *selling*.

"Sales reps shouldn't rely on others for their success, but sales leaders *do* hold a lot of power— they can choose to either make their salespeople's jobs easier or set them up to fail."

John Crowley

FINAL NUGGETS OF KNUCKLE DRAGGING WISDOM

You'll notice that we end here—there are no chapters devoted to actual closing techniques or how to position your product in a presentation.

The reason is simple. Do you know that quote, "Eighty percent of life is showing up?" That's how I feel about sales. In other words:

Eighty percent of sales is getting your foot in the door.

In this day and age, if prospects will sit with you face-to-face, they know you can help them or their business solve a problem. You've done the work to differentiate yourself from a sea of sales reps that lack something you have:

They aren't you.

If you've done your homework and know what your buyers value and what motivates them to act, your presentation can and should emphasize those things. At that point, slick selling and hard closes become a thing of the past.

The "natural-born salespeople" of today are not gimmicky. They don't hard close, hard sell or hard anything else. They don't even feel like they're selling. They simply know how to seek out people who need what they have, and they know how to get it into their customer's hands in a way that's a win for everybody.

The traditional sales cycle is still alive and well. We still prospect for leads, qualify leads, set appointments, make presentations, address concerns, close sales and ask for referrals.

But the traditional ways of going about it are changing.

Decades of "hard sell" salespeople have changed people's appetites and expectations when it comes to buying. We must adapt by approaching buyers with more than our product and our ambition.

We have to give in order to receive. We also have to fight to win.

If you have a lot of quit in you, sales is not for you. If you don't like the idea of being different, sales is not for you. If you're content making $50,000 a year, sales is not for you. Go find a nine-to-five that's less stressful and doesn't require carrying a quota.

The best sales professionals I've been fortunate to work with over the years love the idea of giving to get. Not only does it feel good, but it also pays!

This book is based on my 20 years of experience. I hope you found value in it. If you didn't, I encourage you to email us to disagree and provide your point of view.

These are my opinions, and I'm not a "guru." Like you, I'm just trying to learn. I encourage you to reach out.

As my final tip, from one Knuckle Dragger to another, I'd like to add that the pursuit of money does funny things to some people. I've encountered a disturbingly large number of leaders who encourage members of their sales team to overextend themselves as motivation for "selling more." I've seen too many well-intentioned managers convince optimistic sales reps to go on the lavish vacations and take on the 8,000-square-foot-house mortgage, the Maserati and the Chaparral boat.

There are forces outside our control, such as market collapses, corporate strategy changes and recessions that can leave salespeople stuck with bills they can't afford, eventually leading to the destruction of families.

Reach for the moon in your quest to make seven figures, but until you get there...

I beg *salespeople* not to buy into this false and destructive form of motivation.

I beg *sales managers* not to encourage this destructive behavior.

I beg *sales leadership* to educate their teams on personal financial responsibility rather than hiring "sales reps with big houses and fancy cars."

If you have to use false motivation, you're not a good sales leader. These stressors have caused health issues, divorce and even suicide. It's not necessary. It's not healthy.

Many of us wish we had the biggest cave and the finest fur boots that woolly mammoth tusks can buy. And as I said in the beginning, money (or at least the fear of not having money) *can* be a why, because having financial means gives you the ability to accomplish all the bold, amazing things you want to do in life.

But for what it's worth, my experience is that money in the bank is far more satisfying than money spent on stuff and gone forever.

In the end, I'm just a knuckle-dragging sales guy who's trying to spark a "De-Evolution Revolution" in order to get back to what really works in selling.

Do you have that fighter's spirit? Are you a survivor? Think you could have braved the Ice Age and come out on top?

If you want to find the success you're after, follow the steps in this book:

- Embrace the fear and get your mind right.
- Reverse engineer a small handful of strategic goals.
- Pick your Big Fish and be different to get their attention.
- Learn the business of your customers.
- Utilize Access Selling by engaging with insight and creating value.

Keep on pushing and dragging your knuckles through the fear. Do that, and you'll enjoy a six-figure or even a seven-figure career that speaks to your why and delivers value to everyone you encounter.

Here's to your successful de-evolution,

Big Red

ACKNOWLEDGMENTS

JOHN'S ACKNOWLEDGEMENTS:

Ma, Wara, Bean and Bubbles—Thanks for loving me despite my limitless flaws.

Loves—Thanks for being the big brother I never had and for getting me in more trouble than any big brother could.

Jeb—Thanks for demonstrating that it's possible to be a great family man, businessman, #gainzbrother and terrible fisherman at the same time.

Schwab—Thanks for the long walks in the woods when I thought the world was crashing down and for the motivational bumper stickers.

Rouse—Thanks for opening my eyes to the online business opportunities and the world of animated gifs.

Glinter—Thanks for constantly challenging me, even when I'm right.

Cardinal Family—Thank you for teaching me so much these past four years and driving me to follow my passion for sales.

Jen Lill-Brown—Thank you for keeping me motivated, focused and close-to-on-time during the entire writing process. I can't wait for our next project.

JEN'S ACKNOWLEDGEMENTS:

First, I give all glory to Jesus Christ, my Lord and Savior, for every blessing and ability.

Dad—You get most of the credit for making me the writer and business-woman I am today. Life would not function well without you, Papa.

Will—You are my best friend, reality checker and support system. Thanks for putting up with me and loving me unreservedly.

Mom—You are my other best friend and most trusted source for just about everything. Thanks for modeling what a mom/wife is supposed to look like.

Porter, Wyatt and Jesse—I did not know how much love, joy and pride I could feel until you three arrived! I love life more because of you.

John Crowley—Thanks for believing in me and going "all in" when all you thought you wanted was a blog.

Allison Meek—What would I do without you? No seriously, I mean it! You make my life so much better by being in it.

Ken Abraham—I'll never understand why you gave me a chance, but I will be forever grateful that you did.

James Malinchak—You took my ghostwriting side business and turned it into a full-blown career.

Dr. Josh Axe—Your loyalty and faith in me makes me want to get better and better at my job.

Thanks and love to you all!

ABOUT THE AUTHORS

JOHN CROWLEY

I have been in healthcare sales since my college internship at a generic pharmaceutical company. I dialed for dollars and carried the bag for 14 years. I've sold products as simple as birth control and as complex as electronic medical record (EMR) and integrated delivery systems. I've gone from having no control over pricing as a pharmaceutical rep to having full pricing autonomy as a distribution rep. I've sold "me-too" rubber gloves and novel physician dispensing business models with lucrative revenue streams.

Along the way, I've made countless painful mistakes. I've had periods when I grew bored and stagnant. I've struggled to find work and to even get out of bed in the morning because I lacked purpose. I've doubted the efficacy and safety of my products. I've worked for companies with misaligned compensation plans that rewarded mediocrity over excellence. I've been debilitated by micromanagers and hamstrung by narcissistic executives. I've been sued for millions by a Fortune 50 company over a fallacious non-compete. I've fallen, gotten up and learned from my mistakes.

The one constant through it all has been my unwillingness to quit. In fact, I've been calling myself "just a knuckle-dragging sales guy" for as long as I can remember. As the Vice President of VitalSource GPO at Cardinal Health, a Fortune 26 company, I am fortunate to lead a team responsible for providing pharmaceutical contracting and services to the community oncology and urology physician class-of-trade. We help doctors and administrators run their practice more efficiently so they can spend more time taking care of what matters—the patient. I'm proud to be part of this team and the work we do. We directly impact patient lives, we're experiencing explosive growth and we're doing it differently from our competitors!

One of the reasons I'm so passionate about healthcare sales is because I'm a survivor. I beat lung cancer at the age of 31! During my battle, I experienced the value that physicians, patients and hospitals derive from healthcare sales professionals. Without them, physicians would be undereducated, patients would go untreated and care facilities would be at risk. I may have lost a lung, but I gained an experience that has fueled my success.

Several years ago, I began writing about healthcare sales on my blog, JustJohnCrowley.com, and what started as a side passion has evolved into a business! As a result, I've been asked to speak to dozens of sales teams. I've discovered the rush I get while speaking, and I am grateful that I now have the opportunity to positively affect even one person's life. In 2016, MedReps.com recognized me as one of Healthcare's Top Influencers. Today I speak to sales organizations across the country and have the privilege of helping other knuckle draggers as their sales coach and mentor.

Growing up in New Jersey taught me what it means to hustle. As a kid, I had an affinity for selling. On Scantron test day, I sold boxes of #2 pencils to my classmates for $1.15 (the same price as lunch). I sold white t-shirts from my locker to neglectful classmates who forgot their gym clothes. If I could make money, I jumped at the opportunity. I'm also a proud graduate of The College of New Jersey, formerly Trenton State College.

I'm happily married to my best friend, Amy. We have two beautiful girls, Logan (11) and Keira (9) and live in Brentwood, Tennessee, a quintessential Nashville suburb, with our two mutts, Tick and Jones. When not at gymnastics or school, we are practicing yoga, enjoying the neighborhood pool or cultivating our artistic and entrepreneurial interests. Most mornings, I can be found wearing earbuds and working out while listening to the latest business, leadership or sales audiobook.

JENNIFER LILL-BROWN

When other little girls were playing house, I was playing "business." My father was a sales and marketing professor, a serial entrepreneur and a sales consultant. From the time I knew what selling was, I was destined to be involved in the sales world in some way. But what self-respecting, aspiring businesswoman

goes to college thinking she'll be in sales one day? I certainly didn't, which is why I put all of my energy into pursuing my finance degree at the University of Alabama.

While there, I was approached by a sales organization I knew very well—the Southwestern Company. When I was young, my father had conducted sales training for Southwestern in our hometown of Nashville.

At the age of 10, I had stood on stage with him, in complete awe of all those college kids who worked so hard to make five and even six figures during the summer when other college kids were content to make minimum wage lifeguarding, cutting lawns or dog walking.

The Southwestern Company recruits and trains college students to sell educational books, software and website subscriptions door-to-door. If it sounds hard, don't be fooled. It is *beyond* hard to relocate to another state and knock on doors for 12 hours a day, day in and day out, all summer long.

But I wanted to test myself. So I relocated to the upper peninsula of Michigan and ran my own business at the age of 20. I was chased by dogs, soaked by hours of unrelenting rain showers, had the cops called on me, got my bag kicked off the porch, and was so exhausted that I fell asleep while driving home to the twin bed I shared with my roommate. It was the most difficult thing I'd ever done, but my hard work paid off. I was awarded the "Top First Year Dealer" award at the end of my first summer.

After college, I floundered in a few dead end "desk jobs" until I was given the opportunity to help my dad edit his college textbook on sales called *Selling: The Profession*. He had recently undergone brain surgery, and I was tasked with editing and rewriting this 420-page behemoth in the voice of my father. I suddenly fell in love with ghostwriting—and the love affair has never ended.

I soon met Tom Black, another Southwestern alumnus who was a legend in the company. Since his time in the "book field," Tom had become a giant in the banking industry and successfully took two businesses public. What started out as an interview to be his assistant ended with an agreement to help Tom write his book, *The Boxcar Millionaire*. We also decided to start a sales training company called the Tom Black Center for Excellence.

My journey with Tom led me to meet James Malinchak, a highly regarded marketing expert and coach for public speakers and trainers. James recognized my ability as a ghostwriter and started referring his coaching clients to me. This gave me the nudge I never knew I needed to become fully immersed in the world of ghostwriting.

Fast forward a few more years, and I am now an in-demand ghostwriter who has helped dozens of prominent professionals and public figures put their passions into words. I have also co-authored four professional selling books with my father, including our most recent work, *Cause Selling: The Sanford Way*, which is based on the vision of billionaire philanthropist T. Denny Sanford.

In the fall of 2016, I met John Crowley, who tasked me to help him with his new book. He didn't know what the book would be called, but he knew he wanted to help more salespeople realize the full potential of their sales careers and their lives. And so Knuckle Dragging Sales was born. Now we are on a mission to help people who got into sales for the freedom and the income potential, but who have become frustrated that their paycheck and their lifestyle do not match their expectations.

Today, I can be found working in Nashville surrounded by the sounds of little boys. My husband Will and I live amidst the madness that is raising three homeschooled, amazing sons—Porter, Wyatt and Jesse. My parents, Martha (Grandma) and David (Papa), live right next door and are proud, devoted grandparents to our boys.

SPEAKING AND COACHING OPPORTUNITIES

**Want the Knuckle Dragging Sales Guy
to speak to your organization?**

To find out how to book John
for your next event, visit us at:

WWW.KNUCKLEDRAGGINGSALES.COM/SPEAKING

**Interested in taking your sales career
to the next level?**

To find out more about our
coaching programs, visit us at:

WWW.KNUCKLEDRAGGINGSALES.COM/COACHING